Praise for *The Anxiety, Depression & Anger Toolbox for Teens*

The Anxiety, Depression, & Anger Toolbox for Teens provides a platform for teens and parents to identify the often conflicting emotions experienced during the journey of adolescence. This "toolbox" is a superb resource for teachers and counselors; also Dr. Bernstein's activities help the reader understand the "why" behind the often overwhelming feelings experienced by teens, in addition to the "how" of managing the emotions. I highly recommend this excellent resource for enhancing your pre-teen or teen's emotional intelligence and their communication skills.

—**Sherry Skyler Kelly, PhD**
Clinical Neuropsychologist/Licensed Psychologist,
Founder of PositiviTeens®

Dr. Bernstein is a gifted psychologist and writer who has once again found a way to supply a vast range of useful clinical strategies in a gentle, thoughtful and accessible manner. I am looking forward to sharing many of these ideas, reflections and exercises with my patients, and believe that they will have great relevance and applicability for the countless teens who struggle through the inescapable emotional turbulence of adolescence.

—**Brad Sachs, PhD**
Psychologist and author of *The Good Enough Child,*
The Good Enough Teen, and *When No One Understands*

Dr. Bernstein once again offers practical, insightful tips through his skillful integration of mindfulness, positive psychology, cognitive therapy, and more that is user-friendly and engaging for a wide range of teens and caregivers alike.

—**Chris Willard, PhD**
Clinical Psychologist, Harvard Medical School, and
co-author of *Alphabreaths* and *The Growing Mindful Card Deck*

As teenage anxiety and depression escalate at an unprecedented clip, Dr. Jeffrey Bernstein offers a vital resource of insightful, actionable support. His toolbox of worksheets and targeted, concise guidance helps teens, parents, educators, and therapists flip the narrative of anger and conflict created by academic pressure, home clashes and social issues with friends. You will want to follow his direction to resolve the distress of your adolescents or those you work with so that they can tamp down the stressors that fuel teen anxiety and depression, and gain control of their emotions and lives.

—**Susan Newman, PhD**
Social Psychologist and author of
The Book of No: 365 Ways to Say it—and Mean it and *Stop People-Pleasing Forever*

Written in a voice that young adults can relate to, Dr. Bernstein puts right out there the issues teens are faced with at home, in school, in the media and in the world at large. The activities show teens how to welcome and cope with their daunting realities. By taking deep, focused reflections and using the quick and highly effective strategies that Dr. Bernstein describes, teens can learn how to cope and live happily. I recommend this book to anyone who works with teenagers in any setting.

—**Ivan J. Katz, EdD**
Superintendent of schools, Fallsburg
Central School District, Fallsburg, NY

This little gem of a workbook offers a variety of valuable mindfulness, CBT, and positive psychology skills to help teens learn to manage difficult emotions and prepare them for the obstacles they will inevitably face during the adolescent years. Dr. Bernstein not only explains and shares the tools but also asks the important questions that will get teens to reflect and think things through before reacting.

—**Stephanie Margolese, PhD**
clinical psychologist, and author of *My Brain Team:
What To Do When Emotions Run High* and *Sam's Big Secret: Coping With Fear*

ANXIETY, DEPRESSION & ANGER

TOOLBOX FOR TEENS

150 Powerful Mindfulness,
CBT & Positive Psychology Activities
to Manage Your Emotions

JEFFREY BERNSTEIN, PHD

Copyright © 2020 by Jeffrey Bernstein

Published by
PESI Publishing & Media
PESI, Inc
3839 White Ave
Eau Claire, WI 54703

Cover: Amy Rubenzer
Layout: Amy Rubenzer & Bookmasters

ISBN: 9781683732716

Printed in the United States of America.

PESI
Publishing
& Media
pesipublishing.com

ABOUT THE AUTHOR

 **Dr. Jeffrey Bernstein** is a psychologist with over 32 years of experience specializing in child, adolescent, couples, and family therapy. He has appeared on the Today Show, Court TV as an expert advisor, CBS eyewitness news Philadelphia, 10! Philadelphia—NBC and public radio. Dr. Bernstein has authored six prior books, including *The Stress Survival Guide for Teens*, *Mindfulness for Teen Worry*, *10 Days to a Less Defiant Child*, *10 Days to a Less Distracted Child*, *Liking the Child You Love*, and *Why Can't You Read My Mind?* He has also published the *Letting Go of Anger* therapeutic card deck for teens.

DEDICATION

To Marina for broadening my world and filling it with joy.
And in honor of my late father, Louis, and
to my ever-inspiring mother, Evelyn.

TABLE OF CONTENTS

ACKNOWLEDGEMENTS

Thanks to Karsyn Morse, my acquisitions editor at PESI, for believing in me for this project. And thanks to Hillary Eggebrecht at PESI for being supportive and for encouraging me to submit the proposal for this workbook in the first place. Thanks to Linda Jackson and all editorial staff at PESI for helping to put excellent edits, formatting, and touches on this book. A shout-out of deep appreciation and love to my children, Alissa, Sam, and Gabby, for being awesome in their unique ways and for helping me further understand life from the wonderfully fulfilling perspective that comes with being their dad. And finally, thanks to all the children, teens, and parents I have counseled and coached for well over thirty years for helping me learn and grow, both in my profession and as a person.

INTRODUCTION

This book is written in a teen voice, but it is also for therapists, educators, and parents. Anxiety, depression, and anger are presented together in this workbook because teens frequently struggle with these three very common emotions. The main focus of this uniquely designed workbook is to help you learn to Handle Anxiety (Part A), Cope with Depression (Part B), and Manage Anger (Part C). These commonly experienced emotions for teens—quite strong at times for all of us, of course—are presented as they relate to four big-time challenging areas of your life: school settings, social situations, body-image concerns, and family issues.

Anxiety results from your brain perceiving something threatening. Depression is a looming, persistent sense of sadness and can occur even when things in our lives are seemingly going well. Anger is usually connected to some type of frustration. In your life as a teen, these emotions may seem really far removed from you and then, all of a sudden, they come upon you and you can feel walloped by them! Or you may feel like you struggle with one or all three of these emotions really often and for a long time.

Either way, here is a glimpse of what you will see covered in this workbook to help you cope with difficult times and situations related to school, social connections, body-image issues, and family concerns:

- **School and academic-related anxieties, sadness/depression, and anger** that come from demanding classes, tests, presentations, and homework.
- **Socially-related anxieties, sadness/depression, and anger** resulting from struggles to feel accepted by, and connected and fulfilled, with others.
- **Body-image anxieties, sadness/depression, and anger** that wear on you as a result of being in a culture that emphasizes looks over the value we may have to offer beneath our exteriors.
- **Family-related anxieties, sadness/depression, and anger** resulting from issues and tensions with your parents and siblings.

You will learn to cope with your difficult feelings in these situations using quick, easy, super effective, and *proven* strategies from mindfulness, cognitive behavioral therapy (CBT), and positive psychology skills. As you will see, these three approaches are all effective for managing your challenging emotions, yet each has a different slant. It's not about which one is "the best" but rather which strategies feel best for you at any given time. Briefly, these three ways to manage your anxiety, depression, and anger can be thought of in the following way:

- **Mindfulness Activities**—Help you to focus on what is going on around you and within you in the moment to help notice your concerns without judgment and to help quiet your mind.
- **Cognitive Behavioral Therapy Strategies**—Enable you to evaluate and challenge your upsetting thoughts and replace them with emotionally healthier ones.
- **Positive Psychology Skills**—Steer you toward optimistically focusing on your strengths, and help you gain grit, develop gratitude, and become optimistic, while also learning the empowering feeling of flow (that sense of feeling "in the zone").

These three types of tools can all be used to cope with anxiety, depression, and anger. Whether you use all three of them or, if you prefer, just one or two of them, what is most important is that you keep an open mind when learning them and then find what works best for you. That said, if you prefer mindfulness for one type of emotional struggle, for example, you may value using CBT and/or positive psychology for dealing with upsetting feelings in another situation.

Even though anxiety, depression, and anger are separate emotions, they often run together, occurring at the same time. For example, if you feel super worried about school, you could also feel hopeless or sad, or even lash out in anger at your parents in order to feel more in control. C'mon now—do teens ever really do that? Or, you may feel anxiety so intensely that it leads to depressed feelings, or vice versa.

While anxiety, depression, and anger can occur together at times, they will be presented and discussed separately in this book. Doing so allows for providing specific, targeted skills to help you manage these common emotional struggles, each of which can feel very complex and weighty in its own right.

HOW TO USE THIS BOOK

- It is recommended that you review all of the tools (activities). This is because one area of your life that may seem to be going well now may prove to be challenging in the future, and when it does, you will have knowledge of how to cope.
- Once you have seen all the strategies and considered some examples of situations where they can be used, the parts, sections, and subsections of this workbook can be reread and used in any order.
- Do your best to answer the reflective questions included in the worksheets, and don't beat yourself up if you need to give further thought before coming up with some of the responses.
- Whether you are using this workbook on your own, or with a therapist, try to approach all the activities with an open mind. That said, realize that it is okay to have preferences based on which strategies feel best for you.

Realize that learning new skills and getting good results from them takes time, and the more you practice applying them, the better you get at them.

The Unique Structure of This Workbook

The unique structure of this workbook is to provide you with at-a-glance convenience to quickly access activities to help you manage anxiety, depression, and anger respectively. It provides additional background on each emotion, as well as mindfulness, CBT skills, and positive psychology skills, all of which you can apply either at school with peers, or at home. This workbook will be divided into a total of three main parts:

> **Part A: Handling Anxiety**
> **Part B: Coping with Depression**
> **Part C: Managing Anger**

Within each of the main three parts, you will find tools grouped in:

- **Getting to Know (Anxiety, Depression, Anger)**
- **Mindfulness Activities**
- **Cognitive Behavior Therapy Strategies**
- **Positive Psychology Skills**

In each part, **Getting to Know** provides a brief overview of each of the three emotions—anxiety, depression, and anger. The mindfulness, CBT, and positive psychology discussions are filled with tools that have been proven to lower teen stress.

The **Mindfulness activities** in each part help you become aware of your thoughts and feelings without being so attached and reactive to them. All mindfulness techniques are a form of meditation. *Meditation* simply means focusing your awareness. Mindfulness helps you notice and accept what is going on inside your mind, inside your body, and in the world around you, shifting your focus away from the troublesome thoughts buzzing around in your head. It will help you appreciate joys and notice challenges in life without overreacting to them.

Cognitive behavioral therapy teaches you to identify and challenge unhelpful, counterproductive thoughts and feelings which can make you feel really stressed out and upset. The essence of CBT involves challenging your emotionally upsetting thoughts with more realistic, healthier thoughts. As you practice CBT skills, you'll see how changing your *thoughts* changes your *feelings*, and this helps you change your *behaviors*. Let's say you're riddled with anxiety about your upcoming dance audition. How awesome would it be to transform those thoughts that are plaguing you—thoughts like *"I'll bomb out at this audition!"*— to thoughts that help you feel more confident and encourage you to practice so that you can truly do your best onstage?

A third set of skills you'll learn come from what's known as **positive psychology**. Positive psychology will help you see and appreciate the good things within you and in your life. As you'll learn, positive psychology includes seeing your strengths, learning how to become more optimistic, gaining grit, finding flow (kind of like being "in the zone"), and having gratitude. Grit and resilience are similar, but there is an important distinction. *Resilience* is the ability to adapt in the face of stress, in times of hardship, or in light of bad past experiences. *Grit* is the determination to keep working toward your dreams and develop the skills you need to accomplish even the toughest goals.

In short, as you go through this workbook, you will address how anxiety, depression, and anger are manifested from school, social, body-image, and family circumstances, and how to use mindfulness, CBT, and positive psychology to manage these situations and feelings.

Seeing how mindfulness, CBT, and positive psychology tools have distinctly different approaches to managing anxiety, depression, and anger helps you identify and try out strategies that will help you in any of the areas where you may struggle to find the most helpful tools to apply at any given time. Keep in mind that a particular tool that may not seem very helpful now may feel more so in the future.

Part D is a guide to help therapists use the tools in this workbook for maximum effectiveness with clients struggling with anxiety, depression, and anger who face a range of challenges spanning difficult situations.

I am excited for you to learn how awesome mindfulness, CBT, and positive psychology are for managing your emotions. I'm confident that the skills you gain from this book can help you feel calmer, more focused, and happier throughout your life.

Part A | HANDLING ANXIETY

GETTING TO KNOW ANXIETY

Anxiety is commonly described as a feeling of worry, nervousness, or unease, typically about an imminent event or something perceived as threatening with an uncertain outcome. As a teen in this fast-paced digital age, you are facing more pressures and worries than any generation before you. Anxiety disorders in children and teens are at an all-time high. And even if you, like most teens, may not have an actual anxiety disorder, anxiety is still present in your life.

As you well know, being a teen is not all sunshine and rainbows. Whether it is trying to keep your grades up, staying connected through communication conflicts, dealing with family drama, or certain peers pulling away or you wanting to get distance from them, a whole lot of things can fill you with anxiety if you let it. The bottom line is that anxiety can leave you feeling overwhelmed, alone, and miserable! Making matters worse, the impact of anxiety that is not coped with appropriately can be very serious for you.

Have you struggled, or are you struggling now, with any of the following concerns and worries?

- Experiencing school pressures to get good grades?
- Feeling seriously squeezed on time between school, after-school activities, part-time jobs, and hanging out with friends?
- Getting teased (even if they say, "Just kidding"), put down, or otherwise bullied by others?
- Having peers actively or passively pull away from you because you don't fit in with the "popular group"?
- Feeling like an outsider because of your personal interests, sexual orientation, racial identity, religion, or the gender you align yourself with?
- Experiencing the ups and downs of real-life social connections or social media postings and happenings?
- Feeling socially awkward due to the expectations from within yourself to look cool and at ease in the eyes of your possibly judgmental peers?

In everyday life, when you're in the midst of situations like those described above, you may have a hard time describing what it means when you're are feeling anxious. Just know that even if it is sometimes hard to describe your anxiety, you're not alone. Anxiety can be super confusing to understand. This is because teens and adults call anxiety by different names. Still, however it is referred to, anxiety is the most common mental health problem among teens.

(Note that the terms worried and anxious will be used interchangeably throughout this book.)

Check out the following tools to explore some of the common yet wide-ranging terms that are often used to describe anxiety in these types of situations or others.

WHAT DOES
ANXIETY MEAN TO YOU?

Anxiety presents itself in situations where you feel threatened. One of the most challenging problems about anxiety, however, is feeling that there is something wrong or defective in us for having it. This leads to anxiety about our anxiety!

Underline or circle any words that you may use to describe yourself when you feel anxious:

Stressed Out   Edgy   Uneasy
Nervous   Triggered   Annoyed
Panicky   Basket Case   Frozen
Apprehensive   Worked Up   Alarmed
Freaked Out   Butterflies   Restless
Uptight   Scared   Tongue-Tied

Which of the above negatively viewed words do you tend to identify with most often when you are experiencing nervousness or anxiety?

Worked Up

_____

_____

Which of the above negative words do you hear your peers use (or do they appear to feel) when they are feeling worried?

Uneasy

_____

_____

Describe how the more you are aware of what anxiety means to you, the more you can identify and handle it when it comes your way.

_____

_____

_____

DO YOU HAVE
ANXIETY ABOUT ANXIETY?

Do you ever find that a big challenge about anxiety is not just anxiety itself, but that you get super worried about feeling anxious?

Take a few minutes and reflect on how you react when you notice you're feeling anxious. Fill in any related thoughts that come up for you in response to these negative "anxiety about anxiety" thoughts.

What is wrong with me for being worried about this? (If you have had this thought, where did you learn to see it this way?)

_____

_____

_____

Being anxious makes me feel so weak and defective. (What societal, peer, or family views lead people to think this?)

_____

_____

_____

What if I can't stop being so worried all the time? (How does this thought fuel existing anxiety?)

_____

_____

_____

What if those kids can tell that I am totally freaking out inside my head right now? (Why do we feel we need to cover up and hide when we feel anxious or vulnerable? How can this thinking make us even more anxious?)

_____

_____

_____

I'll never get to enjoy my life because I worry too much. (Why is it unfair to ourselves to have a negative outlook about the things we struggle with?)

_____

_____

_____

EXPLORING
SHAME ABOUT ANXIETY

It is important to understand that shame-related descriptions for anxiety are actually barriers to dealing with anxiety. Before you begin to learn ways to cope with anxiety, ask yourself if or how any of these problematic negative associations of anxiety have gotten in your way, or your peers' way, of facing anxiety and working through it.

As you reflect on the following words below, think about situations in your life where your anxiety left you feeling in ways such as these. Circle any of these negative anxiety associations that you may at times have experienced.

Loser	Lost	Negative
Weak	Wimp	Deficient
Defective	Babyish	Useless
Left Behind	Inadequate	Inferior
Not Fitting In	Unworthy	Embarrassment
Messed Up	Burden to Others	Not Cool

Which, if any, of the above negative terms have you ever associated with anxiety?

_____

_____

_____

Did you experience these feelings in any particular setting or with certain people? For example, in class, with peers, or with family members?

_____

_____

_____

Why do people see having anxiety as something negative?

_____

_____

_____

Which of these words have you heard your peers use about themselves or about others facing challenges related to anxiety?

_____

_____

_____

How does it seem to impact you when peers, family members, or others you know express shame and other negative feelings about having anxiety?

_____

_____

_____

How can anxiety be made worse by seeing it in a negative way vs. seeing it as something you can work on and overcome?

_____

_____

_____

Does it help to realize that successfully handling your anxiety does not mean that you have to get rid of it?

_____

_____

_____

Explain how the more you take the pressure off yourself to think you need to be worry-free in order to enjoy your life, the more relief and joy you will feel right away.

_____

_____

_____

ANXIETY ABOUT ANXIETY

Reflect on the following questions to help further explore situations where anxiety about your anxiety just makes it feel worse.

When I get anxious around other people, I tend to beat myself up by saying this to myself:

_____

_____

_____

If a school assignment or test is really hard or overwhelming and I feel worried, I can be super hard on myself by saying:

_____

_____

_____

If my skin, hair, or body does not look the way I want it to and I feel self-conscious, I make myself even more miserable by saying this to myself:

Opportunities in my life that I have lost because of my anxiety include:

_____

_____

_____

SEEING THE IMPACT OF
ANXIETY TRIGGERS

Let's briefly explore the specific situations (triggers) when anxiety pops up the most and least in your life. Rank (from 1 to 8, with 1 being your most common trigger and 8, your least) the following situations where you get the most anxious:

_____ School assignments or tests

_____ Body-image concerns

_____ Fitting in socially

_____ Family conflicts

_____ Fear of something bad happening to you

_____ Fear of misfortune happening to someone you know

_____ Fear of something bad happening in the world

_____ Fear of failing

_____ Other: _____

What did you learn about yourself by ranking the situations that trigger your anxiety?

_____

_____

How can identifying different things you feel anxious about help you to manage them better?

_____

_____

Are the relative ranks of the situations that currently make you feel anxious the same as one year ago? Five years ago? Do you think that, one year or five years from now, the ranking of what makes you feel anxious will likely change? If so, how? Reflect below.

_____

_____

MAKING "PIZZA"

WITH YOUR ANXIETY TRIGGERS

Another way to see the relative impact of various situations as triggers for your anxiety, and to find PEACE, is to think PIZZA! Consider the image below as eight slices of pizza. Take a look again at the rank-order list on the previous page. Which triggers of your anxiety could you put on pizza slices (or even half slices) to account for the total anxiety you feel at this time of your life? To help you see this, simply write down on the slices those sources of anxiety you ranked in the previous tool. It is likely that any of the triggers may take up more than one slice. For example, maybe your current social concerns account for a slice and half, and your school pressures take up four or even more slices of the overall anxiety in your life. Don't get too hung up on trying to be super "slice precise." The main point of this exercise is see the relative impacts of various sources of anxiety that you may struggle with.

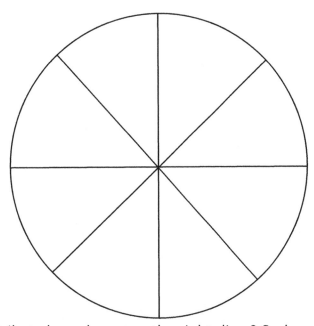

Are your worries distributed evenly among the eight slices? Or do one, two, or three of the things you worry about fill the whole pizza?

_____

_____

Based on looking at this "anxiety pizza," what is your biggest stressor (source of anxiety)?

_____

_____

Are you surprised to see how much or little certain stressors create anxiety for you? If so, what thoughts and feelings does this lead to for you?

_____

_____

_____

How is it helpful to see this chart that represents where your anxiety comes from?

_____

_____

_____

UNDERSTANDING YOUR ANXIOUS BRAIN

So far we have discussed how anxiety is overwhelming, how it's seen in a negative way, how it gets covered up, and where it pops up. Now let's take a closer look at anxiety to really understand what happens in your brain that leads to your worries in the first place.

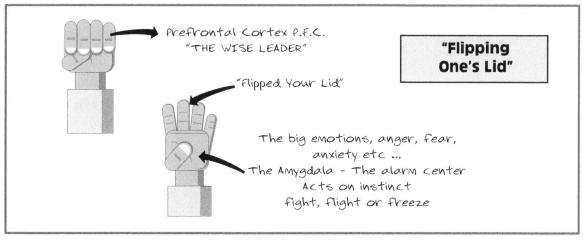

Adapted from Dr. Daniel J. Siegel's Hand Model of the Brain found in *Mindsight: The New Science of Personal Transformation* (Bantam Books, 2010)

There is a "hands-on" way, so to speak, to understand anxiety in your brain. The hand model of the brain developed by Dr. Daniel Siegel shows you what goes on inside your brain, including when you feel anxious.

Bend your left elbow and hold your left hand in front of you at eye level. Now make a fist (with your thumb on the inside of your palm), keeping it at eye level (have no fear, I'm not going to ask you to punch yourself as a new trick to help you stop worrying). Keep your hand in place as you read on.

Your "Primitive Brain" or "Reactive Brain"

Your wrist represents your spinal cord, and as it comes up to your hand it becomes your brain stem, which is also called your *hindbrain*. The hindbrain is the most basic and, evolutionarily speaking, the oldest part of the brain. It controls breathing, heart rate, and blood pressure, and it gives you your survival instincts. Now look at your thumb. Your thumb represents the limbic system, which sits on top of the hindbrain.

The limbic system is the place where we hold, store, and integrate memories of fear and where we experience other emotions. The amygdala, an almond-shaped set of brain cells in this region, allows us to react quickly to things we feel threatened by or are afraid of.

The limbic system and hindbrain work together to initiate the "fight, flight, or freeze" response that is so important to our basic survival. If—as early humans sometimes did—you suddenly meet a fierce-looking tiger, only one thing matters to your life in that instant: your ability to fight it, run away from it, or play dead in hopes that it will ignore you. If you're like most teens, in your day-to-day routine there are not many potentially fatal threats lurking around corners. So instead you dread getting slammed with reactive brain thoughts toward situations like these:

- A ton of homework ("*I'll never get this done!*")
- Feeling awkward or insecure around a new group of people ("*What if they think I'm a loser?*")
- Letting your secret crush see you on a bad hair day ("*I'm gonna lose any chance of him noticing me!*")
- Your parents giving you a hard time about you wanting to go hang out with a particular group of friends who they feel is not a good influence on you ("*I'll never get to be with my real friends!*")

It's as though *these* things might be just as disastrous to your health, well-being, or hopes for the future as a tiger attack. Pretty unrealistic, right?

Your "Thinking Brain"

Still looking at your hand? Good. Your fingers represent the top and front part of your brain. This is your prefrontal cortex, the evolutionarily newer, higher part of the brain. Your prefrontal cortex allows you to perceive the outside world and to think and reason. It also regulates the feelings in your lower brain—when your lower brain raises an alarm, your cortex can tell it, "Stay calm" or "Let's get out of here!"

When you are feeling uncertain about school pressures, peer or family stress, or your secret crush, especially if you are tired or someone pushes one of your emotional buttons, you can end up "flipping your lid" (lift up your fingers from resting on your thumb to see a representation of "flipping your lid"). When this happens, the crucial thinking and reasoning frontal part of your brain goes "off-line." This is also known as "freaking out," "flipping out," or "losing it."

What all this means is that if you are really feeling stressed, scared, or angry, your cortex—your thinking brain—loses the ability to control your knee-jerk emotional and physical reactions. At those times, your worries really get the best of you, and you may try to resist (physically or verbally) or run away from whatever is making you feel so upset. You may end up saying or doing things you later regret. Or you may simply freeze—for example, you find yourself unable to speak or to begin working on something you need to get done.

GRASPING YOUR THOUGHTS:
THE HAND MODEL OF THE BRAIN

How does the hand model of the brain help you in understanding your anxiety?

_____

_____

_____

Now that you are considering this model, what things can you do to help keep your prefrontal cortex in charge of your reactive brain?

_____

_____

_____

When your prefrontal cortex, thinking brain, stays in charge or regains control from your reactive brain, it can lead you to say things that help you cope and gain hope. What are some positive coping thoughts that your thinking brain has led you to say or do to manage your anxiety in the past?

_____

_____

_____

What are some past situations that you avoided or that did not go well for you because you were not considering that your anxiety was coming from within your reactive brain rather than from what was going on around you?

_____

_____

_____

YOUR MIND-BODY CONNECTION

After learning where anxiety comes from in your mind, it is now helpful to see how anxiety can find its way into your body, where it can really take a toll. As you will also see, learning to identify what is going on in your body as stemming from your anxiety can help you manage these physical signs. And tuning in to what is going on inside your body can help you become more aware of the anxiety that is occurring within your mind.

If you tend to experience physical symptoms when you worry, these symptoms themselves likely give you cause for concern. And the more concerned you get about the sensations in your body (not to mention your concern about whether people can see that you're worried, especially if you have social anxiety), the more your mind has to worry about. This can lead to an unhealthy cycle of being too absorbed in your body and letting it influence your mind. The following illustration shows how worried thoughts influence your body's reactions and how these reactions, in turn, can lead to more worries.

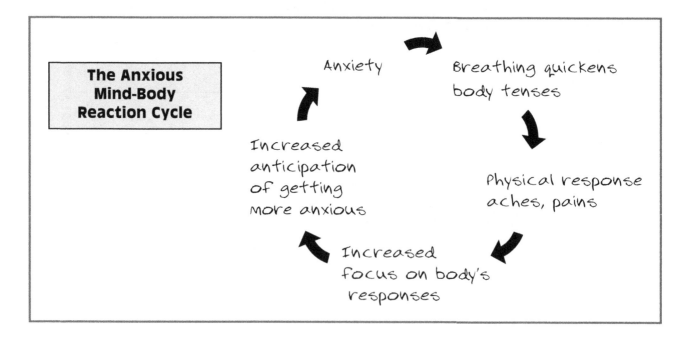

As you can see, worries can affect your mind and body in a way that makes you more upset. Now let's take a closer look at how, when anxiety gets stuck in your head, worries can create aches, pains, and other problems in your body.

WHEN ANXIETY SHOWS UP

Unfortunately, we only tend to see anxiety showing up in our bodies as a bad thing. But when we tune in to our bodies and notice that anxiety may be appearing, we can use this as a way to cue us to manage it.

Circle any of these physical anxiety symptoms that your experience at times. Add other symptoms on the blank lines.

Tightness in Your Chest	Shaking Hands
Tightness in Your Throat	Voice Quavers
Neck Ache	Pounding Chest
Sweaty Palms	Nausea
Backache	Dry Mouth
General Muscle Tension	Sleep Problems
Butterflies in Your Stomach	Headache
Faster Breathing	Sweating All Over

_____   _____

_____   _____

_____   _____

ANXIETY CAN MAKE YOU PHYSICALLY ILL

Can you see how physical reactions related to anxiety could take a toll on your health over time? And so you may ask, "Why are our bodies wired to react this way to begin with?"

In order to survive, your prehistoric ancestors had to decide whether to fight, flee, or freeze when facing a saber-toothed tiger. This fight, flight, or freeze response, which is a function of your reactive brain, causes your body's nervous system to release stress hormones. These hormones get you ready for action, which can be tremendously helpful in the short term.

Over the long term, however, consistently high levels of stress hormones (one result of excessive worry) can negatively affect your nervous system, your organs, and your glands. The more stressed your body becomes, the worse you feel. Chronic, severe worrying, otherwise known as anxiety disorders (described in the following box), can lead to headaches, stomachaches, sleep issues, physical illnesses, and depression.

Manageable Anxiety vs. Anxiety Disorders

We all feel anxious at times. This workbook provides activities that can be used to help manage your normal, manageable worries as well as severe, persistent worries that cross the line to become an ongoing mental health problem. It is recommended, however, that you do see a mental health professional if you have a more severe form of anxiety, as will be described in this section.

How do you tell the difference between common, everyday worries and more intense anxiety disorders—where is the line? Well, daily worry (and higher levels of it from time to time) creates mild-to-moderate emotional distress, whereas anxiety disorders tend to create severe emotional distress, to the point of not being able to function effectively. Common teen worries can bring on some of the same physical symptoms as anxiety disorders, but to a much lesser and more manageable degree.

You may wonder with great concern whether you have an anxiety disorder. The term "anxiety disorder" means that your worrying has become so extreme that it can be hard for you to make it through the day and even lead a normal life. This type of disorder is serious, compared to the common bouts of worry that every teen struggles with from time to time. If you have an anxiety disorder, your worries and fears are higher than normal and may seem to be almost never ending.

Some teens with anxiety disorders worry so intensely that they avoid going to school or even appearing in public for fear that something bad will happen. Although there are several kinds of anxiety disorders, they all have some common symptoms. These include feelings of panic, dizziness, problems sleeping, cold or sweaty hands or feet, difficulty breathing, a racing heart, an inability to be calm, nausea, muscle tension, and tingling in the hands or feet.

The most common anxiety disorders that can affect teens are:

Panic disorder. People with panic disorder get surges of intense fear that seem to hit them out of the blue. These alarming episodes make them feel frozen. When teens with panic disorder describe these episodes afterward, they say things like: "It's really scary. My chest was pounding, and I felt like I couldn't breathe." Or "I just froze up." Some even say that it felt like they were "going crazy." Usually the panic is triggered by being in a certain type of situation. For example, one of my clients felt very self-conscious whenever he would break out in a sweat, so much so that he spiraled into panic.

Social anxiety disorder. People with social anxiety disorder experience huge worries and feel super self-conscious about everyday social situations. For example, they feel as though everyone is looking at them and judging them negatively, even though they know deep down that this may not be true. Teens with social anxiety disorder usually worry about being seen as losers or outcasts. Or they are constantly on edge about doing something that causes them embarrassment or shame.

Specific phobias. These are intense fears of specific things or situations—fears that are usually way out of proportion to those things or situations. Phobias lead people to avoid ordinary situations such as sharing the street with dogs (if they have a phobia of dogs) or going to the top floor of a building (if they have a phobia of heights).

Generalized anxiety disorder. People with generalized anxiety feel stressed out almost constantly. They describe feeling as if their anxiety switch is stuck in the "on position"— even when there's nothing around to trigger it. Their worries are over the top and cause a lot of tension.

If you think you may have an anxiety disorder, or if your worries are accompanied by depression or by intense, hard-to-manage feelings, please see a qualified mental health professional in addition to using this workbook.

One way to help prevent manageable levels of anxiety from becoming full-on anxiety disorders is to learn to recognize anxiety so that you can then cope with it. Let's look at how anxiety that is felt in your body can cue you to identify any associated thoughts and feelings in your mind. Check out the next tool, which has a table to help you explore your body-mind anxiety connections.

DISCOVERING YOUR
MIND AND BODY TRIGGERS

Anxiety Triggers	My Upsetting Thoughts	Where I Feel It In My Body
School Pressures		
Social Situations		
Body-Image Issues		
Family Concerns		
Other		

What did you learn by identifying where anxiety shows itself in your body and how it relates to your thoughts in response to different triggers?

_____

_____

_____

What patterns, if any, do you see in how your anxiety shows up in your body and thoughts across different triggering situations you face?

_____

_____

_____

How can recognizing your bodily symptoms of anxiety help you be less anxious about having anxiety in the first place?

_____

_____

_____

DO YOU COPE IN
DESTRUCTIVE WAYS?

It is easy to fall into managing anxiety in unhealthy ways too. Take a look at each of the ways described below and share a situation where this may have occurred for you or someone you know.

Pretending your anxiety does not bother you and ending up on the "bottle it up and explode (or implode) later plan." For example, you might hold your anxiety in and then yell at someone or throw something when feeling overwhelmed (more on this later when we discuss anger).

_____

_____

_____

Blaming others (teachers, parents, friends) for problems and having this make anxiety worse and harder to manage.

_____

_____

_____

Getting sucked into the distractions of unkind gossip and drama, excessive social media use, video games, or using substances to escape from worry-related struggles.

_____

_____

_____

Using avoidance (procrastination, refusal to go places, school-attendance issues) to escape from facing triggers of anxiety.

_____

_____

_____

WORRYING CAN COST YOU

Seeing the counterproductive and potentially harmful ways of managing anxiety, consider the following questions:

What are some of the lost opportunities and periods of time that worries have taken from you?

_____

_____

_____

What are the emotional costs of undealt-with worries you have experienced (sadness, anger, fatigue, hopelessness)?

_____

_____

_____

Describe how worries get in your way (at home, in school/sports/other activities, or with peers).

_____

_____

_____

On the more positive side, what are some things you are doing now that you did not do before because you overcame certain worries (e.g., sleeping without a light, providing a food order to a server, asking a teacher for extra help)?

_____

_____

_____

JUST STOP WORRYING—YEAH, RIGHT!

Has anyone ever said to you something like, "You just need to stop worrying!"? If so, did it really help? Have you ever demanded of yourself that you stop worrying? I doubt *that* worked for you either.

This notion of "thought-stopping" backfires because it forces you to pay extra attention to the very thoughts you want to avoid. You always have to be watching for them, which makes these unpleasant thoughts seem even more important.

Let's now talk about how you manage your anxiety at school. I wouldn't blame you for having the fantasy that you can just make school attendance totally optional, get rid of homework, be allowed to hang out all day with friends, and have the smartest kids do the classwork for everyone else. That would sure make for less school stress—but we know that is not happening!

So how about just chilling out with the next sections to learn how to feel calmer about school?

We are going to start with mindfulness, which helps you notice what is going on inside your mind, inside your body, and in the world around you, shifting your focus away from troublesome thoughts buzzing around in your head. But before we start mindfulness, let's talk right up front about a seemingly huge obstacle to it—distractedness!

Ignoring Distracting Worried Thoughts Is Like Trying Not to See a Pink Giraffe

Sometimes teens tell me that trying to ignore distracting thoughts when practicing mindfulness is like trying not to notice a pink giraffe standing in front of them. I respond to these frustrated teens by saying, "I understand! I often experience the same struggle!" When they hear that I, too, have trouble with distracting thoughts, they gain confidence in their own ability to be as mindful as anyone else. Mindfulness is not something that anyone does perfectly.

It is common to wonder, "Can I really be mindful and less anxious with my distracted, racing mind?" The short answer is yes! Don't believe me? Then take the Pink Giraffe Challenge in the next tool and answer the follow-up questions.

SEEING BEYOND
THE PINK GIRAFFE

Part 1. Close your eyes. Imagine, as vividly as you can, a bright-pink giraffe. Yes, bright pink! Visualize a very large pink giraffe with a long, pink neck. Make the giraffe start dancing.

Part 2. Okay, now close your eyes and try *not* to think about the pink giraffe. Don't think about how big it is. Try not to think about it reaching up so high with its super long neck. Make yourself think of anything else but the pink giraffe. Keep doing this for a few minutes.

At the end of a few minutes, what are you thinking of? During those few minutes, how many times did the pink giraffe cross your mind? Quite a few?

Part 3. Okay, now close your eyes again. Tell yourself that for this next part of the exercise, it doesn't matter whether you think about the pink giraffe. Your goal now is to gently focus your attention on noticing your in breath and out breath, your bodily sensations, and the sights and sounds around you. Do this for a few minutes.

How many times did you think of the pink giraffe this time? None? Maybe once or twice?

Can you see how trying to force yourself to think (or not think) about something is not helpful? Yet when you allowed yourself to accept that you may have thoughts about the pink giraffe, you likely stopped pressuring yourself to exert control over your thoughts. This accepting attitude helped you mindfully notice your breath, your body, and the sights and sounds around you. The pink giraffe likely no longer dominated your thoughts in the same way and began to fade into the background of your mind.

The pink giraffe exercise is intended to help you realize that you can be mindful even when you have distracting thoughts. These include non-anxious thoughts, such as, "What will I eat for dinner?" and worried ones, such as, "Did I fail my math test?" Just as you learned with the pink giraffe, being preoccupied with thoughts you *don't* want to have is bound to backfire. Accepting your distracting thoughts and gently refocusing yourself feels so much better, and is much easier, than trying to stop or control your thoughts. By the way, if you find yourself never getting distracted again in your life after taking a few mindful breaths, then please contact me immediately to help me write a very thin, new version of this workbook!

The capacity for mindfulness is already within you. You don't have to go to the top of a mountain or deep in the woods to practice mindfulness. You can do it just about anywhere you are. Doing just a few minutes of mindfulness activities a day, or even a few times a week, and seeing yourself and the world around you in a mindful way will result in your worries being less frequent and less intense. Your willingness, patience, imagination, attention, and breath are the only things you need to make mindfulness work for you for the rest of your life.

MINDFULNESS FOR SCHOOL ANXIETY

Mindfulness will help you appreciate joys and notice challenges about school without overreacting to them. Mindfulness means being in the present moment. The big problem with school-related anxiety is that it's based on events that have not happened yet. Can you see how your mind goes way into the future when you worry about things at school? Disruptive anxiety about tests you have not yet failed, anticipating being embarrassed before you even answer a question in class, or worrying about not being able to do your homework before you even start it are all examples of anxiety being a land of fiction. That's because the outcomes you worry about have not happened yet—and may never happen. By practicing mindfulness, you can learn to appreciate the positive things about school and notice your academic challenges without overreacting to them.

Mindfulness is easy to learn, once you understand what it really is. Some people have misunderstandings about mindfulness. When they think of mindfulness, they associate it with fully enlightened, blissfully happy Buddhist monks without a worry in the world, as portrayed in movies (unrealistic movies, that is). Maybe some people even think that mindfulness involves holding crystals containing special powers to escape the feelings of everyday stress. Before we go further, let's take a look at what mindfulness is and what it is not.

Mindfulness Is . . .	Mindfulness Is Not . . .
noticing your thoughts and sensations that help you and upset you at school.	making your mind a "blank slate" or stopping all thoughts.
having awareness of your breath, body, and mind in the classroom and in school-related tasks.	a mysterious technique that takes years to learn and can't be used anywhere but on a mountaintop.
noticing what is going on in the moment.	achieved only by meditating for hours at a time.
re-centering yourself to cope and gain hope.	sitting and drowning in worries or misery.
reacting to school and other worries in a different way.	learning to never worry again.

Okay, now that you have a sense of what mindfulness really is, let's get into more detail about how it will help you manage your school-related anxiety.

MINDFULLY EXPLORING
SCHOOL WORRIES

Just imagine yourself being anxious about school. Reflect for a few moments, just noticing what you are thinking without being attached to these thoughts and feelings. As you now have a sense of what has passed through your mind, please answer the following questions:

Describe school situations that trigger your anxiety (e.g., tests, teachers, being called on, hard projects, etc.).

_____

_____

_____

On which days of the week and at what times of the day do you get most anxious?

_____

_____

_____

What types of school-related anxiety did you have in the past that you now do not struggle with as much, if at all?

_____

_____

_____

How does worrying about school-related demands make them worse for you?

_____

_____

_____

How could your efficiency at getting things done be improved by noticing your anxiety-related thoughts without reacting to them in the same way?

_____

_____

_____

MINDFULLY EXPLORING YOUR WORRY

As you go forward, just try to be open-minded and patient. The mindfulness exploration activities and meditative tools in this book are the ones that teens I know have found most appealing and helpful. The amount of time you spend "staying in" and repeating the activities throughout this book is up to you. Do what feels comfortable, and gently encourage yourself to do a little more if you're willing. Now let's talk about how awesome your breath is when it comes to mindfulness.

Your Breath Is an Anchor for Mindfulness

Breathing mindfully is an effective way to manage your worried mind, which is why it's part of many exercises throughout this book. Noticing your breathing is a centering and reliable way to focus on what is going on in the present moment, and considered an anchor for mindfulness. Since you have to breathe all the time anyway, why not take time to breathe mindfully every day? Making mindful breathing part of your daily routine will go a long way toward helping you feel less stressed. Let's briefly highlight why mindful breathing, when done correctly, will be a helpful part of managing your school-related and other anxieties.

Being in the present moment shifts your awareness away from the worries in your head and quiets your mind. By focusing on your breath, you bring your awareness to the present moment—the cornerstone of mindfulness. One way to breathe mindfully is to simply notice your breath as it is: notice without judgment whether it's fast or slow, shallow or deep. You may certainly do all the exercises in this book in that manner.

I encourage you to gently extend your in breaths deeper into your belly, all the while keeping an attitude of nonjudgment. This is because deep, mindful "belly breathing" increases the supply of oxygen to your brain, helps you think more clearly, and signals your body to relax. This happens because your breath is part of a feedback loop with your nervous system.

When you're on edge—agitated, excited, or scared about a pop quiz or that fast-approaching deadline on a paper—you breathe quickly and shallowly. This type of breathing, called chest breathing, helps your body prepare for action. Your heart rate and blood pressure increase, and you feel more alert to potential dangers. This cause-and-effect relationship works in the other direction, too: when you breathe quickly and shallowly, you feel more on edge. Try it and see. It's certainly hard to relax while breathing this way, isn't it?

Compared to chest breathing, when your breath flows into the lower part of your lungs (did you know your lungs extend all the way down below your lowest ribs?) and you expand your belly like a balloon (referred to as belly breathing), it stimulates your vagus nerve, which extends from your brain down into the organs in your abdomen, including your heart, lungs, and stomach. What's really cool about this is that your vagus nerve is part of a group of nerves that help shift you *out* of stress mode. By activating your vagus nerve, beginning with your first deep belly breath, your heart rate slows, your blood pressure drops, and you feel more relaxed.

Think of a car racing down the highway at 120 miles an hour. That's you in stress mode, and your vagus nerve is the brake. When you are super anxious, it's as if you're pushing the gas pedal to the floor. Slow, deep, mindful breaths can become your trusty brake pedal.

To learn mindful breathing with deeper breaths, as described in the next activity, place one hand on your chest and one on your belly (below your rib cage and above your belly button). If you're at school and want to take some belly breaths, which will likely help you when you're feeling stressed out, you probably will want to be a little more subtle and not have your hands on your chest and belly.

But for learning this cool way of breathing, the belly-chest hand placement really helps you—literally, you *are* your breaths!

BREATHING IN
CALM FEELINGS IN CLASS

As you gently breathe in, focus on drawing your breath in through your nostrils, noticing how it feels as it passes through your trachea and down into your belly. Then as you reverse this process, imagine your school-related worries leaving you as you breathe out. You will notice that, with each breath, the hand on your chest moves only a little, while the hand on your belly more noticeably rises with each in breath and sinks down with each out breath.

This is the opposite breathing pattern of rapid, chest breathing, which is how we tend to breathe when we're worried. For maximum effect, silently remind yourself that you're breathing in and out, and tell yourself what you are trying to achieve in a few simple affirmations. Here is a sample of what you can say to yourself while doing this exercise:

Breathing in, I am feeling calmer.

Breathing out, I am releasing my anxiety about school.

Breathing in, I breathe in new energy.

Breathing out, I release tiring school worries.

How did this breathing exercise feel for you?

_____

_____

What was it like to release your school anxiety through your breath?

_____

_____

How can focusing on your breath in the present moment help you gently shift from worrying about future school-related outcomes?

_____

_____

FLOATING AWAY SCHOOL WORRIES

Notice the space below, which shows some leaves on the page. Now reflect for a few minutes on things that make you anxious about school. Think about those homework assignments and tests, that Monday-morning anxiety (ugh!), difficult projects, or nerve-wracking presentations. Now write one or more of those scary stressors on the leaves.

Okay, now imagine these school worries floating away on a stream. What was it like to imagine your worries floating away and letting them go?

_____

_____

_____

Now consider those leaves in the stream changing into stepping stones that allow you to cross over the water. Using the picture below, write some coping strategies on the stones that will help you cross this stream of school stress. For example, these stepping stones may represent creating a homework time schedule, seeking help from a teacher, or focusing on past school accomplishments that can empower you to step past your current anxiety.

How did this leaf visualization feel for you?

_____

_____

_____

Can you see how letting your school worries float away on leaves can help you gain a sense of letting go of them?

_____

_____

_____

How does the image of stepping stones help you feel centered and anchored amid the turbulent demands of school?

_____

_____

_____

TEST WORRIES

Now let's talk tests. Tests are a big-time source of anxiety at school, so let's give them a little more mindful attention in the following activity to help you manage your angst about them. Getting a handle on your test-related anxieties can help you now, whether you're in middle school or high school. If you go to college, you'll find lots of tests waiting for you there as well. And often jobs require employees to take tests.

When test anxiety comes your way, your muscles get tight and even jittery in response to your reacting brain getting all sorts of alarming, counterproductive thoughts. It can be very hard to study or think clearly during an exam (picture that blank page just staring at you) because your overheated thoughts make your mind race! Reflecting on the following questions can help slow down your soaring thoughts about tests.

MANAGING YOUR BODY'S
REACTIONS TO TESTS

Take a few gentle breaths and reflect on a past test experience that was particularly anxiety-provoking for you. Reflect on the surroundings of the classroom at the time. Notice how you felt sitting in your chair with your desk in front of you as you were moments away from beginning the test.

How did you feel in anticipation of this difficult test?

_____

_____

_____

Did you feel alone or connected to the classroom, the teacher, and the material you were about to be tested on?

_____

_____

_____

What happened in your body when you experienced anxiety over this test?

_____

_____

_____

Now take a few deep breaths and imagine your anxiety over this test riding along and away from you on your out breaths. How does this feel compared to how you felt answering the questions above?

_____

_____

_____

PREPARING FOR PRESENTATIONS

If the thought of doing a class presentation is really scary, rest assured that you are not alone. But by using some mindfulness strategies, you can make any presentation less painful and more successful. If you approach your presentation efforts with a beginner's mind (having curiosity about the material to help feel connected to it and to the presentation experience), prepare properly, and know your topic well, you may actually enjoy doing presentations. At the very least, the process will feel more tolerable. Keep the following tips in mind for making presentations a more pleasant experience:

1. Before your presentation, visualize where you will be giving your talk. During this reflection, picture your worries drifting out the door from which you entered the room. (You can also proactively practice this and all the following steps even if you don't have a presentation coming up at this time.)

2. Take several deep, long, relaxed breaths before you begin your presentation.

3. Notice and gently resist any urges to rush. It is common for worried teens to speed through a presentation to get it over with, but rushing it can heighten your anxiety.

4. To avoid rushing, share your information in a spirit of curiosity, as though you were just learning about it yourself. This will help your audience focus more on your topic instead of how you are presenting it. If worries come your way, gently take a breath and reconnect to a calmer state.

5. Even though your peers probably have no choice but to listen to you, try to have appreciation for their attention. You may want to begin your presentation by thanking your peers for their attention. This can help you feel more confident and ease your worries.

How can doing this exercise help your confidence for getting past presentation jitters?

_____

_____

_____

Can you reflect on a time when a presentation of yours, or possibly someone else's, may have gone better if you or they had taken the steps described above?

_____

_____

_____

CBT FOR SCHOOL ANXIETY

Cognitive behavioral therapy is based on the idea that there is a clear link between thoughts, behavior, and feelings. The main points about CBT to keep in mind as you practice it are these:

- Just because you have a thought doesn't mean that what the thought is telling you is true.
- Your stress comes partly from the way you interpret events, not just the events themselves.
- Questioning your unhelpful, inflexible thoughts and replacing them with more reasonable ones can help you feel less stressed out.
- Thinking in more-realistic ways about the struggles you face can help you find better ways to cope with them.

Below is an example of the relationship between anxious thoughts, feelings, and behavior relating to school.

Anxious Thought: I must be stupid because I can't figure out this math homework, even though I thought I knew how to do it when the teacher explained it in class.

Negative Feeling: Anxious.

Problematic Behavior: Avoid doing the homework and don't turn it in.

This connection of thoughts, feelings, and behaviors can be seen as cyclical, as shown in the graphic below.

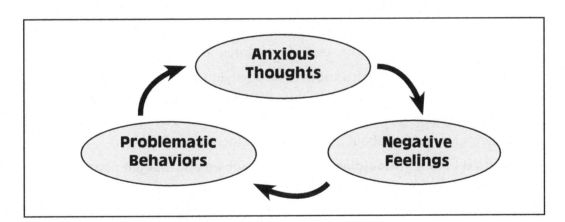

As suggested by the diagram above, the teen who thinks he is stupid avoids doing schoolwork. Then when he doesn't get it done and fails to turn it in, his belief that he's incompetent is reinforced. As you can see, the student in this example branded himself with the negative label of "stupid," which got in the way of completing his homework.

In CBT the idea of taking an otherwise-reasonable thought (in this case, "Hmm, this math homework is kinda tough") to a super exaggerated, unhealthy place in your mind, as presented above, is referred to as *cognitive distortion*. Some experts in CBT also use the term *ANTS (automatic negative thoughts)*, which means the same thing. Whether you want to think about them as ANTS, cognitive distortions, counterproductive thoughts, or something else, it's important to realize how these troublesome thoughts are usually inaccurate, rigid, and exaggerated.

Check out the following list of common distorted, counterproductive thoughts that can feed your anxiety. (They also often lead to feelings of depression and anger, which we will cover later in the book.)

Common Distorted Thoughts Among Teens

The process of reevaluating and challenging our problematic thoughts—the essence of CBT—is sometimes referred to as *cognitive restructuring*. While these problematic ways of thinking (that is, cognitive distortions or ANTS) are discussed here in the anxiety section of this workbook, they will apply to the depression and anger sections as well. They include:

- **All-or-nothing thinking:** Otherwise known as polarized thinking, this type of cognitive distortion comes into play when we think things in our lives have to be perfect or else we are just a failure. So, for example, if you don't get an A on that test then you unfairly see yourself as a total failure.

- **Jumping to conclusions:** This occurs when we fool ourselves into thinking we can read others' minds. As an example, you may already think that you will be seen in a negative way at a party before you even get there.

- **Negative filtering:** This occurs when we focus on the negative aspects of a situation and exaggerate or magnify them while failing to see any positives. For example, your teacher says you did a nice job on a presentation but also provided constructive feedback with the suggestion that you slow down your pace. You then dismiss how well you did when the teacher really just wanted to hear what you had to say.

- **Catastrophizing:** This is also known as magnifying or minimizing. Catastrophizing occurs when we say things to ourselves like "What if," where we expect the worst things to happen. For example, you might say, "What if I don't make the baseball team and kids give me crap about it for the rest of the year?"

- **Should thinking ("Shoulding"):** With this problematic thought pattern, you have a list of rigid rules about how you and others should behave. Let's say you're frustrated about how long it's taking you to do a single math problem. You may problematically think, "What is wrong with me? This math problem shouldn't be so hard to do." Sometimes teens, and even adults, think that beating themselves up with the word *should* makes them feel or look noble. The reality is that it leads to shame. And shame can lead you to feel down, and zap your motivation to get things done and reach your goals.

- **Negative labeling:** You rigidly stick a negative label on yourself. When it comes to schoolwork, teens frequently saddle themselves with unfair labels like "lazy" or "stupid."

- **Negative comparisons:** This occurs when you unfavorably compare yourself to others. For example, you may think, "She's thinner, and she's prettier, so who cares if I have nicer hair?" Or, "He is a star athlete and hot girls like him; who cares if people think I'm smart?"

The following exercise will help you start learning how to battle your own distorted thoughts. CBT does take some practice because we typically go through our days not paying attention to how we can automatically make ourselves miserable. But hey, if I could give you a completely effortless, sustainable way to lower anxiety, then I wouldn't have written this book. Instead, I'd be hanging out on one of the many islands I'd own, because countless people would have paid me to instantly change their thinking patterns without any work. Nice fantasy, but not reality!

Learning to identify these unhelpful thoughts gives you the ability to question and challenge these counterproductive beliefs to stop them from getting in your way.

Exploring Your Unhelpful, Counterproductive Thoughts

Just think about how some of the negative, counterproductive thoughts that you have about tests, presentations, and homework demands can trigger certain worries. You can probably agree that those upsetting thoughts get in the way of these academic demands. But when you use your CBT skills, you'll see that just because your reactive brain leads you to doubt your academic abilities, that doesn't mean you have to buy into these worried thoughts.

In following up on the illustration and example on page 35, let's now focus on distorted, problematic thoughts and how to counter them with more helpful, reasonable thoughts.

For example, if you were to think a counterproductive, all-or-nothing thought like, "I will never understand this homework chapter," you might reframe it with a helpful thought, such as, "Yeah, this chapter is tough, but I have made it through hard class material before."

If you have a negative labeling thought like, "I failed the science test, so I am stupid," you might consider replacing this with a more positive thought, such as, "I didn't do well on this test, but that doesn't mean I'm stupid. I get better grades when I study more."

If you have a "shoulding" thought like, "I should have studied harder for the math test tomorrow," a more realistic, reasonable alternative thought would be, "I'm not loving this hard math test, but I'm willing to give it my best effort."

If you were upset and had a negative-comparison thought such as, "Why did I get a C on that lab assignment when my partner got an A?," you might feel a lot better by thinking, "I did my best, and I even improved from last time."

Okay, now it's your turn to start battling those weighty, distorted thoughts that get in your way by making you anxious about school.

DISPUTING AND REPLACING
UNREALISTIC THOUGHTS

You will see a table below with an example to start you off. The first column, "Negative Thoughts about School," is where you can write down negative thoughts. In the second column, labeled "Reframed, Helpful Thoughts," write down a more helpful thought on the subject in the first column. The third column is "Type of Cognitive Distortion." You may experience different cognitive distortions at the same time. In this activity, try to fill in the table with your own negative, distorted thoughts about school and the type of distorted thinking represented by each one.

Negative Thoughts about School	Reframed, Helpful Thoughts	Type of Cognitive Distortion
I just can't learn chemistry.	Even though it is hard for me, I'll get further if I try my best.	Jumping to conclusions

Did identifying your own counterproductive school thoughts and coming up with new and helpful thoughts increase your confidence (a healthy, helpful feeling) in your ability to manage and meet these challenges (by taking healthy actions) in school?

_____

_____

_____

Does challenging your counterproductive self-doubts with more helpful thoughts seem like a good way to break free of them and be ready to do your best?

_____

_____

_____

Now simply reflect on whether writing more helpful thoughts increased your confidence (a healthy, helpful feeling) in your ability to manage and meet your challenges? Journal your thoughts below.

_____

_____

_____

CONQUERING SELF-LABELS
THAT LEAD TO SCHOOL WORRIES

We will look at varying types of cognitive distortions throughout this workbook. The thought distortion illustrated earlier on, "I failed the science test, so I am stupid," is referred to as *negative labeling*. All of the counterproductive thinking patterns described earlier can create anxiety about school for you. But now, with the next tool, let's take a zoom lens to examine a sticky one in particular—labeling.

Take a few moments and reflect on times when you have given yourself a negative label about your schoolwork that ended up getting in your way. Some common negative labels teens may put on themselves include: "lazy," "stupid," "dumb," "incompetent," or "less than." Which not-so-flattering labels about school, if any, have you given to yourself at times?

_____

_____

Has unfairly labeling yourself and any resulting negative feelings ever gotten in your way with your schoolwork? If so, what happened?

_____

_____

Do you have peers whom you have observed being really hard on themselves by referring to themselves with such negative labels? If you have ever experienced this, or could imagine this happening, how might it affect you to see others give themselves a negative label?

_____

_____

What do you think happens to the motivation of those who trash themselves with negative labels?

_____

_____

Now let's crawl over to one thing that, due to anxiety, many students struggle with, something I just can't put off discussing any longer—procrastination!

A Special Note about Procrastination

Have you ever put off studying, homework assignments, long-term projects, and, if you're a high school senior, college applications? Has avoiding your schoolwork (perhaps in favor of going on social media, messaging your friends, or playing video games) ever led you to a lot of worries, aggravation, and even all-nighters? Have you maybe even taken out your procrastination-related anxiety on your siblings or parents? If so, you're a card-carrying member of the Procrastination Club. This is one club no longer worth paying your dues to!

If you procrastinate, perhaps it's out of fear of not doing your schoolwork perfectly. Maybe you feel overwhelmed and stressed out from too many demands, so you rationalize that you "deserve" time to relax. Maybe you've counterproductively told yourself that you hate school, that you "just lack motivation," or that you're a "hopeless" procrastinator. Or maybe you try to tell yourself, vaguely believing it, that you'll "do it later," when you feel more up to it—but that time never comes.

Let's use some CBT skills to find motivation to help you quit procrastinating.

LOWERING YOUR ANXIETY

BY TAKING ACTION

Think about the illustration showing the cyclical relationship between thoughts, feelings, and behaviors. Negative actions toward school (e.g., procrastination) follow negative thinking (e.g., "I'll never be able to learn this!") and negative feelings (e.g., frustration, hopelessness). This leads to counterproductive actions/nonactions (shutting down and avoiding schoolwork).

By taking some different actions, however, you can lead yourself to some healthier thoughts and feelings to get you back on top of your school challenges.

Put a check mark next to the coping behaviors that can help you be more motivated about school.

____ Ask for help.

____ Get better sleep.

____ Make up a schedule for when to do your homework.

____ Make up a list of necessary tasks, and then put check marks beside or cross out the things you complete to reinforce yourself for doing them.

____ Set aside your electronic device when sitting down to do your work.

____ Set a timer for five minutes to activate yourself. (You can "constructively lie to yourself"—tell yourself you will only do five minutes of work and then, once you are into it, see if you're now willing to do more.)

____ Remind yourself of past projects you resisted at first but then pushed yourself to get through.

____ Ask yourself how you will feel afterward if you engage in the work you need to do.

YOUR FOUR-WORD
MOTIVATION FORMULA

Still concerned about your procrastination keeping you stalled out for schoolwork?

To get moving on your school demands, here is a simple four-word magic formula for you: "I'll do it anyway!" What is so cool about making this expression your mindset is that you don't have to "be ready" to approach stressful challenges. Here's what makes this a great way to "unslump" yourself:

I'll puts you back in the driver's seat to claim responsibility for what you will do.

Do redirects your thinking to accomplishing the task or goal instead of continuing to lose sight of it.

It focuses you back on the specific task to be done.

And what about **Anyway**? This word creates a huge motivational influence because this "allows" you to have resistance yet also push through it to act and get things done! This inspires grit.

Even if you aren't completely feeling it, you can still do something that is in your best interest. Here's how you can apply this:

- If you get distracted and now don't want to study, that's okay, but thinking "I'll do it anyway" will allow you to accept your resistance without you giving in to inertia.
- As you get flooded with thoughts that, for example, you can't do your written project for English class, telling yourself "I'll do it anyway" helps you bypass your resistance.
- If you are feeling intimidated about asking your teacher for help, thinking "I'll do it anyway" can empower you to do so.

Now try to write below three to five school-related demands that you don't want to do, and then practice saying, "I'll do it anyway."

_____

_____

_____

_____

_____

CARING VS. WORRYING ABOUT SCHOOL

As strange as this may sound, school-related anxiety can give some people a false sense of security. Worrying can lead you to feel as if you're able to remember important things, can make you feel more motivated, or even can seemingly help you to succeed.

Caring about your concerns, however, is a far more helpful and productive use of your time than *worrying* about them. When you care about your needs, your goals, certain situations, or certain people, you're hopeful that things will go well. Caring keeps you from wasting energy by worrying. It helps you focus on doing what's important to you rather than avoiding what makes you uncomfortable. It helps you stay healthy and is good for your relationships with your family and friends.

This powerful and helpful shift from worrying to caring is a cool way to reframe what you're anxious about at school—or in any situation, for that matter. You can feel really freed up emotionally by realizing that you are not giving up your concerns by giving up the *urge* to worry. Once you unshackle yourself from the urge to worry, you'll be able to cope with your anxiety in a calmer way. Now let's go to school and try to make this work for you.

REFRAMING SCHOOL:
ANXIETY AS CARING

Drawing from the following list of caring phrases, try filling in the blank caring statements that follow the worry statements.

Invested In

Keeping an Eye On

Doing My Best

Working Toward

Giving My Best Effort

Committed to Studying for

Paying Attention to

Being Aware of My Effort

Being Dedicated to

Making It a Point to

Valuing My Efforts to

Being Open to

Planning to Make Progress On

Learning from My Mistakes

Seeing Myself Catching On

Being Patient with Myself to

A reframing of a worry statement to a caring statement appears below. After you check it out, try to come up with your own caring statements as alternatives to the worry statements appearing below.

Example:

Worry statement: "If I don't feel worried and scared about this math test, then I will just fail it. There's so much I have to do—ugh!"

Caring statement: "This math test matters a lot to me, and I am committed to preparing well for it. But getting myself worked up will waste the time and energy that I could use to prepare for it."

Now try your own hand at reframing worrying into caring:

Worry statement: "I'm freaking out overthinking that I will not be able to get into a good college."

Caring statement: _____

_____

Worry statement: "When I worry, I shut down and get behind in school, and that just makes my anxiety worse. Then I get further behind and the anxiety is even worse. Wow, I just suck at life!"

Caring statement:_____

_____

REWRITING AN ANXIETY STORY

Now let's further practice your CBT skills for school by helping Sam rewrite his anxiety story, below, as a story of caring.

Anything felt better to Sam than schoolwork demands and a test he wanted to avoid preparing for, because thinking about it left him feeling stressed out. So he lost himself on astronomy websites and his other pastimes—video games and social media.

Unfortunately, by avoiding his schoolwork and test preparation, Sam let his unchallenged negative self-talk lead him to feel anxious, which he unfortunately was unable to work through. Sam's avoidance through video-game screens then left his anxiety unresolved *and* ended up making the situation worse.

Check out Sam's self-defeating thoughts below, and help him out by filling in the blanks.

Sam's teacher reminded the class about an important science test that will be given in a few days. Sam starts to think, "I'm going to fail this test." A more helpful thought for Sam might be:

"_____."

Sam gets even more anxious, and then a flood of additional worries comes to him. He finds it super hard to stop thinking to himself, "I am not only going to fail this test, but I will probably now fail the class for the year." Instead of this he could have thought:

"_____."

This led to an even worse thought, which was, "I'm doomed. I'm just too freaked out and scared to freaking even know where to begin!" As an alternative to this he could have thought:

"_____."

You may not realize this, but by rewriting Sam's story, you saved him from his past tendencies to be overpowered by his worry-laden thoughts and feelings about failing this big test. He tried to escape his stress by playing video games and spent a lot of time on social media.

Now that you helped him think more caring thoughts, what are some healthier behaviors for coping that you could also suggest for Sam to use?

_____

_____

_____

POSITIVE PSYCHOLOGY FOR SCHOOL ANXIETY

Positive psychology includes really cool concepts such as seeing your strengths, learning how to become more optimistic, gaining grit, finding flow (kind of like being "in the zone"), and having gratitude. To be clear, grit and resilience are similar, but there is an important distinction. Having *resilience* helps you to stick it out when dealing with stress and hard times. *Grit* is not only about staying committed to hard challenges, but also about developing the skills to attain them.

The next few tools include some positive psychology activities that you can use to lower your anxiety related to school. Positive psychology is all about dwelling in what feels good and goes well. The more you do that, the more you will feel empowered to tackle the challenges you face in school.

GETTING SCHOOLED ON
YOUR ACADEMIC STRENGTHS

Do you ever take time to positively view your talents, qualities, and accomplishments in school? It is easy to feel discouraged when an assignment, test, or quiz does not go well. Viewing your strengths creates a "can-do" attitude, which helps you gain optimism and confidence to push through challenges and overcome them.

Take a few moments and reflect on what your strengths are in school from the list below.

Math	Asking for Help	Honesty
Originality	Enthusiasm	Good Communication
Perseverance	Reliability	Practical
Problem-solving	Trustworthiness	Flexibility
Reading	Creativity	Organization
Social studies	Discipline	Detail-Oriented
Sports	Patience	Solid Listening
Strong Work Ethic	Quick Learner	Open-Mindedness
Teamwork	Motivation	Caring
Writing	Determination	Leadership
Geography	Dedication	See the Big Picture

Now consider the following questions to help you reflect on your strengths:

How does it feel to get in touch with your strengths?

_____

_____

_____

Which ones do you have?

_____

_____

_____

What accomplishments are you most proud of, and which strengths helped you achieve them?

_____

_____

_____

When in your life did you lose sight of your strengths, which may have helped you cope?

_____

_____

_____

How can knowing your strengths help you use them in the future?

_____

_____

_____

49

LETTING ANXIETY FLOW TO A
POSITIVE SCHOOL EXPERIENCE

Now let's go with the flow to help you with another way to manage school anxiety with positive psychology. When you're "in flow," you're so into whatever it is you're doing that you might lose track of time, or the outside world might seem to fall away. Your attention is entirely wrapped up in the moment, and the benefit is that for a while you get a much-needed break from your anxiety about school.

Close your eyes or focus your eyes on a spot in front of you. Begin reflecting on a past school experience that you felt really absorbed in and committed to. Maybe it was a book you found hard to put down that related to a historical event you were reading about for social studies. Perhaps, while doing a presentation for science, you knew you were nailing it. Maybe you had a paper due for language arts and time just disappeared as you got into the flow of finding your references, developing an outline, and writing the paper.

What did that absorbing, positive school experience feel like for you?

_____

_____

_____

How did you get yourself in the groove to be so engaged in that particular task?

_____

_____

_____

What are the benefits of being in flow when you have work to do?

_____

_____

_____

How can recognizing when you are in flow help you access more of this productive state of being for other school responsibilities?

_____

_____

_____

GAINING GRATITUDE AND
LOSING SCHOOL ANXIETY

Now let's look at the power of gratitude for lowering your school-related anxiety. Whoa, hold on! I realize that if you are currently struggling with school demands, you may think I am really off my rocker, so to speak, for asking you to be grateful for school. But if you keep an open mind while going through the next tool, you just may discover something cool and helpful about what gratitude can offer you to manage school anxiety.

Just consider for a moment: is your education something you can find gratitude for? Let's reflect on this question with a few other guiding prompts to consider below.

If you really got to just stay at home all day and not be enrolled in any kind of school program, would your life feel better? Perhaps you may feel an immediate sense of relief for no longer having immediate school demands in your face or others looming in the distance. But wouldn't you start to feel bored without the structure of school to keep you feeling a sense of routine and engagement in the world?

Reflect on peers, teachers, or other school staff—who gave you a sense of comfort just by being there? Can gratitude for their calming influence help lower your anxiety?

_____

_____

_____

Consider some difficult school material you mastered even though it was initially difficult to learn. Does feeling grateful for your ability to learn and carve out new ways to think seem like something of value to you?

_____

_____

_____

Can you see how welcoming gratitude into the way you view school demands can help you lead some of your school anxiety to the exit door?

_____

_____

_____

MINDFULNESS FOR SOCIAL ANXIETY

You likely have a strong need for joining with others and probably want to feel as if you belong and fit in with your peers. It's a great feeling to connect with others and know that they care about you. Feeling accepted and understood by friends helps you get through rough times. Let's use some mindfulness to help you feel freer from the common weightiness of social anxiety that can be an obstacle for connecting with others and feeling good while doing so.

BEING MINDFUL OF
YOUR FRIENDSHIP NEEDS

Take a few gentle, soothing breaths in a quiet, comfortable place, and reflect on the following to help you explore your friendship-related needs in a nonjudgmental way.

What are you drawn to in connecting with certain peers who share your interests and views on life?

_____

_____

What are some reasons you may want to turn to friends instead of family members for support when you feel worried or upset?

_____

_____

How do you show trust and loyalty, and what do friends do to show trust and loyalty to you?

_____

_____

How does having social connections and friendships give you a sense of independence?

_____

_____

How do your peers and friends help you develop a personal style that is all your own?

_____

_____

In what ways does feeling similar to your peers keep you feeling close to and accepted by them?

_____

_____

In what ways do you value being different from your peers?

_____

_____

You probably also want to be viewed as popular, cool, and accepted—to look as though you have it totally together. Otherwise, you may worry, other kids might judge you harshly. And they might not do it to your face; they might gossip about you on social media. Thus, the fear of looking awkward, "messing up," being put down, not being liked, or even being abandoned can really feel overwhelming. And what about dating and relationships?

These concerns about how others see you can make you feel super anxious and overly focused on being your best self for everyone else. But by using the power of mindfulness, and sending positive caring intentions to others, you will get away from feeling like you are drowning in a sea of anxiety-fueled self-absorption. Rather, you will feel like, and be seen as, a floating buoy of calm and support for yourself and others.

LOVE AND KINDNESS

Take a few breaths. As you breathe in and out, picture the faces of your friends. Let the care and value you see in them arise before your mind's eye (drawing from your experiences and feelings about them to enhance the mental image). Reflect on their faces with gratitude as you appreciate what each of them brings to you and teaches you. Feel the positive energy you gain from having them as your friends. Now close your eyes and take a few mindful breaths and imagine sending a wave of caring, supportive energy to your friends. Feel your heart beat with joy while reflecting on the gift of your friendships.

Do you feel as if there's more caring energy in your heart to help your friendships thrive and survive?

_____

_____

_____

How might tuning in to the value of your friendships help you feel lower social pressure from others? How about from within yourself?

_____

_____

_____

Now try doing the same exercise as above while focusing on the faces of people you see around but don't know as well.

Do you feel there is more openness and acceptance for those whom you have not gotten close to?

_____

_____

_____

How can this energy help you feel more in harmony with those you are not as close to, even if it is only within your mind? Also, does this energy help you feel less socially anxious?

_____

_____

_____

STAYING CALM IN THE STRONG CURRENTS OF SOCIAL MEDIA

Social media offers you amazing opportunities to connect with friends and others. It's fun and exciting to see what's happening online, make connections, and have people respond to your posts as well as you responding to theirs. What teen doesn't like getting "liked"?

At the same time, social media can springboard teens into the abyss of anxiety. Seeing posts from friends and other peers can trigger both positive and negative thoughts and feelings. For example, you may feel happy for a friend who posted an achievement she was proud of . . . but also feel left out when seeing pictures of her at a party you wish you had been invited to. Or, wouldn't it suck if you see your best friend's recent ex posting a picture of himself with a new girlfriend (or boyfriend)—and you know that it might devastate your friend. Another upsetting situation might be seeing the way that one of your friends is virtually ignored on social media. Or maybe someone you really don't get along with or have a hard time trusting is now edging into your social group, and you're worried about the effect that might have on your circle of friends.

Now let's discuss keeping yourself centered when you are struggling with the faces you see that are not live in front of you but rather on the screens you are looking at when surfing the not-always-gentle waves of social media.

SOCIAL MEDIA
IN A NONJUDGMENTAL LIGHT

Take a few deep breaths, and have a mindful spirit of gentle curiosity as you log in to your favorite social media site. Stay tuned in to what you are thinking and feeling. Note how you are feeling physically (are you tense, or are you loose and relaxed?) and emotionally (are you feeling eager, insecure, worried, calm, valued, or deflated?). If anxiety comes up—about a status you posted that no one's liked, or a party someone invited everyone in your clique to except you—stay mindful and be in the NOW. I use this acronym to mean: **Notice**, **Observe**, and be **Willing** to let things go. Let's NOW look at social media in a nonjudgmental light.

N: **N**otice your value as a person and feel pride about the joy you bring to others in your life.

O: **O**bserve how, while social media expands your social experiences, it can also create anxiety.

W: Be **W**illing to let go of any anxiety you may feel as you reflect on social media by repeating the following:

Social media is just one part of me as a socially connected person. It does not define my value as a person.

Can you see how having a more mindful approach to social media helps you avoid impulsively posting something or responding in a way you would likely have later regretted?

_____

_____

Does taking time to be less reactive to social media give you more time to meaningfully process what you see?

_____

_____

Can being more mindful as you view social media keep you less likely to adopt a distorted view of yourself?

_____

_____

In much the same way, being mindfully aware when you send text messages to others offers a valuable gift of "quality control" to ensure that you write what you mean and mean what you write.

MINDFUL MESSAGING

Reflect on having a "Ready, Set, Go!" intention for messaging, which means not rushing your response (e.g., impulsively responding with a "Go, Set, Ready" mindset). To help you do this, think of a time when you responded in a "Go, Set, Ready" manner and later regretted it. What happened?

_____

_____

_____

Here's something you can try the next time you receive a text message:

Center yourself with a few mindful breaths (a count to ten is usually helpful) and focus your senses on a pleasant image in your surroundings to give yourself a pause in which to create a healthy, reflective frame of mind. Use this mindful pause to message back thoughtfully as opposed to impulsively.

Was this experience easy or challenging for you?

_____

_____

_____

Did you feel less pressure than usual to respond quickly?

_____

_____

_____

Can you think of a downside to being more mindful before you respond to text messages?

_____

_____

_____

CBT FOR SOCIAL ANXIETY

The first step in using CBT for managing your socially anxious thoughts is learning more about what they are related to. If you recall, you got to know your general anxiety triggers back in the tool where you made "pizza" (page 11).

If you're now hungry to get mindfully in touch with how anxiety comes from social situations in your life, then you'll be happy as we turn again to pizza! The following "pizza" consists of "toppings" of the eight common social-anxiety-related thoughts you may face, to varying degrees. Use the following tool to get a sense of which, and how much, these social stressors affect you.

SLICING UP YOUR
SOCIAL STRESS PIZZA

Check out this list of social stressors (the toppings that can push your anxiety over the top):

- Frequent self-doubt
- Upsetting thoughts of being left out or lonely
- Unhelpful beliefs related to not being included in the popular group
- Upsetting reactions to jokes taken too far, being teased and bullied
- Ruminating about gossip that may or may not be true
- Negative self-beliefs related to drama or pressure from a dating relationship
- Counterproductive misunderstandings and conflicts
- Being upset over being left out of social media connections

Now take a few breaths, close your eyes, and visualize the following pie chart. Keeping this mental picture in mind, try to fill in the slices of your social anxiety pizza with any combination of these eight concerns. You may feel that being socially self-doubting creates eight slices worth of stress for you. Or maybe you fill in two slices for a dating relationship, two for a lost friendship, and four for the stress of gossip. Perhaps you'll allocate one slice to each of the eight listed stressors. Just know that there is no one way to do this activity. You may even want to do it now, and then again in a week, and see if your social-stress pizza changes or not. Once you have completed this visualization, fill in the actual slices on the picture you see below.

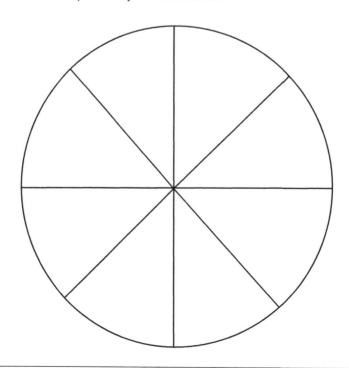

Looking over the eight slices, reflect on how your social stressors are represented by them.

How does it feel to see where your social stress comes from?

_____

_____

_____

Can you notice how some socially anxious concerns may take up way more space than others?

_____

_____

_____

Do you see that how you filled out this pie chart now may have been different a few weeks, months, or years ago?

_____

_____

_____

How does it help to look at the degree to which certain social concerns impact you?

_____

_____

_____

Perhaps you feel that something is wrong with you when you look at areas where you may struggle socially. Just know that this is one common pizza that all teens share. Particular social demands that are especially challenging to you, however, may not be so for others. But then, of course, you may feel less socially stressed in certain situations that are more difficult for your peers.

Knowing you have areas where you may feel socially uncomfortable does not mean you are weak. Actually, acknowledging your social stressors is a huge step in managing them. By the way, if you think all your peers are "fine," then you are likely only seeing them on the surface.

WHEN "FINE" APPEARANCES MAY BE DECEIVING

Do you feel social anxiety by focusing on how some teens may seem to give off that vibe of "It's all chill and I never worry over what other people think of me?" This could lead you to negatively compare yourself to them, thinking there is something inadequate (negative label) with you. But hold on. All those "I'm fine" people are probably secretly thinking and feeling FINE in a not-so-glamorous way:

F: Foolish, Frustrated, or Freaked Out

I: Insecure, Insignificant, or Invisible

N: Nervous, Neglected, or Not Enough

E: Embarrassed, Emotional, or Empty

The pressure on people to look FINE, like they have it all together, is enough to make them feel like they could fall apart at any given moment if their hidden, inner anxiety gets the best of them.

Now here is a healthier way to let FINE represent how you are coping with social anxiety:

F: Freeing up your feelings of anxiety and managing them.

I: Inspiring yourself by being real and knowing your value (as we discussed earlier in the NOW).

N: Not forgetting that everyone struggles, at times, with socially related anxious thoughts.

E: Empowering yourself by challenging your negative self-doubts with more helpful, realistic thoughts.

How about I give you a free hall pass right now so that you can go to an imaginary cafeteria to do the following FINE exercise?

SELF-TALK

AT THE LUNCH TABLE

Imagine that you've been sitting with a group of friends at lunch for the past few months, but now you're beginning to feel like they are losing interest in you. You want to talk, but don't really know what to say. Yet at the same time you feel the urge to start pulling into yourself by shutting down and saying less. You're now thinking that these kids are wondering why you are still hanging out with them, since you don't talk. Now your anxiety is really spiked!

Go through each of the counterproductive thoughts below, checking off the ones that are similar to what you might be feeling if you were the one suddenly feeling more socially anxious at this lunch table.

_____ "They all look so confident and I'm a mess."

_____ "I'll never fit in."

_____ "I should always know what to say."

_____ "I can make friends but I can never keep them."

_____ "I can't really trust anyone."

_____ "I guess I'm just a loser."

_____ "It's a hopeless situation."

_____ "I suck at this."

Now challenge those unhelpful, self-sabotaging beliefs by putting a check mark beside each healthier thought that can replace the unhealthy one:

_____ "Just because they look confident does not mean I can't learn to feel surer of myself."

_____ "Part of fitting in anywhere is accepting that I don't have to be perfect."

_____ "So what if I feel uncomfortable? I still have good things to offer."

_____ "It really helps to remind myself that they doubt themselves at times, too."

_____ "The more I work on knowing my own value, the more others will see it, too."

_____ "It helps to remind myself of times when I have connected well with others."

TAKING ACTION

Remembering that CBT is about thoughts, feelings, AND behaviors, let's get you taking action at the lunch table now that you've centered yourself with some more helpful, empowering thoughts:

Take a deep breath, reflect on being assertive, and engage your peers in a "less-is-more" way, such as smiling, making a supportive comment, or laughing at a joke and then adding relevant brief comments and questions. To help you accomplish this, put a check beside some of the following short samples of conversational bites that seem helpful to you.

_____ "Hey, what are you guys doing this weekend?"

_____ "What do you think of that new music album just released by _____?"

_____ "Hey, maybe this is random, but just saying . . . what would you guys do if you won a three-million-dollar lottery?"

_____ "I heard you killed it at the cheerleading (or soccer, basketball, debate team, etc.) tryouts."

_____ "Yeah, that teacher was hard on me too, but I learned he's cool if you get to know him and ask him about his dogs."

_____ "My sister started working there and she thinks it's a pretty easy job to learn, too."

_____ "Yeah, that new video game update is really awesome."

If you foresee that you'd still have persistent thoughts of feeling uncomfortable with this group, then would you consider whether these thoughts are valid?

_____

_____

_____

Could it be that your thoughts are more about who *you* really are rather than whether *they* accept you as FINE? (Remember that FINE can be positive or negative depending on how you see it and feel it.)

_____

_____

_____

If you decide that it's time to leave this friend group, realize that forming and deepening friendships can take some detours, but you can choose to move in a different direction.

What would be the challenges for you if you were to leave this friend group?

_____

_____

_____

How might you shift your energies to befriend other peers (e.g., sitting with them at lunch, joining new activities or clubs, starting conversations with new people, supplementing your school life with community-related doings such as volunteering)?

_____

_____

_____

WHAT IS THE WORST THING THAT COULD HAPPEN?

Lauren wanted to try out for the school play, but when she thought about trying out, she became filled with self-doubts. Her school counselor told her to ask herself what was the worst thing that could happen if she tried out. When Lauren discussed this further with her mom, she really liked how Lauren's counselor got her to reflect on the worst thing that could happen.

If you look back at when we first discussed catastrophizing, you'll see how "what-ifs" are the typical beginning of these types of counterproductive thoughts. Lauren's "what-if" was: "What if I make a fool of myself up there on that stage?"

Her mom asked her to think about the chances of that really happening. After all, Lauren had been encouraged by some friends to try out. She had also been in the school choir and had experienced being onstage. In fact, a few years earlier Lauren had even done a solo that had been very well received by both students and staff at the school. Then there was also Lauren's full-out enthusiasm for trying out for the play! With these affirming considerations in mind, she felt herself becoming less anxious and more likely to have a successful audition. Lauren realized that just by asking herself, "What is the worst thing that could happen?" the odds of her bombing the audition was highly unlikely.

Now let's look at how thinking the worst in anticipation of social situations can be dealt with by answering the following seven-word question (there is also a different seven-word question which we will use in the anger section later in this workbook).

SEVEN WORDS TO COMBAT
SOCIAL "WHAT-IFS"

Close your eyes and reflect on the "what-ifs" that you have struggled with in the past and those that still come into your mind. Fill in the "what-ifs" blanks below. Reflect on each "what-if" and think about how it gets in your way. Then, counter them with: "The worst thing that can happen is . . ." Can you see how these "what-ifs" can really get your mind racing—but how you can also slow them down with CBT?

Here's an example to help you complete this activity.

What if this new group of friends I want to be part of rejects me at the party I am going to?

The worst thing that could happen is I feel slighted and disappointed, but then I'll also know they are not for me.

What if _____?

The worst thing that could happen is _____

_____.

What if _____?

The worst thing that could happen is _____

_____.

What if _____?

The worst thing that could happen is _____

_____.

What if _____?

The worst thing that could happen is _____

_____.

SEEING SOCIAL
SUCCESSES AND STRENGTHS

When you focus on your positive qualities and personal strengths, you realize you can use them to cope with stressful social situations. Viewing your strengths creates a can-do attitude, which helps you gain optimism and confidence to push through and overcome interpersonal challenges. Focusing on your strengths helps you gain a sense of grit to get back up when you feel anxiety knocking you down.

Inwardly reflect on your past positive social connections and successful times to regain a sense of personal strength and confidence. Write down some of them here.

_____

_____

_____

What social accomplishments are you most proud of, and which strengths helped you achieve them?

_____

_____

_____

Now take a few moments and reflect on things you've done well or can do well in your social life based on the following list of strengths. Check mark your strengths to get you in touch with even more of the good stuff you may see about yourself that you offer to others.

_____ Flexibility	_____ Patience
_____ Ability to Accept Feedback	_____ Loyalty
_____ Enthusiasm	_____ Honesty
_____ Reliability	_____ Easy-Going Personality
_____ Trustworthiness	_____ Good Communication Skills
_____ Creativity	_____ Practicality

Now consider the following questions to help you reflect on your strengths:

How does it feel to take a few minutes and get in touch with your strengths?

_____

_____

_____

When, in a social situation, did you lost sight of the strengths that may have helped you cope?

_____

_____

_____

How can knowing your strengths help you use them in future social situations?

_____

_____

_____

CALMING SOCIAL ANXIETY
WITH OPTIMISM

What are all the things you have to gain by pushing your comfort zone in the social realm? Could it be that you just haven't given these positive possibilities enough consideration? What is the upside you can see right now from challenging yourself to confidently rise up socially to bust free from the confining shackles of your anxiety? Put a check mark next to each one that seems to apply to you, and underneath write in some further benefits related to each one:

____ Feeling less dragged down by fear of failure in the social realm

_____

_____

____ Discovering deeper and more meaningful connections with others

_____

_____

____ Creating new memories by getting out of your comfort zone and mixing it up with others

_____

_____

____ Feeling more empowered to connect with others in the future

_____

_____

____ Discovering you have less social anxiety as you put yourself out there more to connect with others

_____

_____

FINDING YOUR
FRIENDSHIP GRIT

Part of being friends with someone is not only enjoying the good times but also being able to support a friend or feel supported by them when either of you has to deal with hard times. That takes grit.

What is a challenging situation that you either shared with a friend or that they shared with you?

_____

_____

How does being supportive or feeling supported by a friend strengthen you and build confidence in your ability to make solid connections with others?

_____

_____

How does weathering the tough times that go on in a friend's life, or having your friend be there for you in rough times, help you feel less alone and less anxious?

_____

_____

Why is it important to value the depth of your friendships and not just the number of friends you have?

_____

_____

How can helping an acquaintance lead you to a path of friendship with that person and, in turn, lower your anxiety?

_____

_____

MINDFULNESS FOR BODY-IMAGE ANXIETY

Body image refers to how you view and feel about your physical self and how you believe others view your appearance. If you often get caught up in worries about how you look, then learning to manage these upsetting feelings can really help you feel better. Mindfully valuing your face, body, or any aspect of your physical self from the inside is a way to feel love and compassion for yourself, as well as to feel calm and relaxed, which will help with your worries.

The following quote speaks to the immense feelings of relief from anxiety we can feel when we mindfully look at our bodies with acceptance and love:

> And I said to my body softly, "I want to be your friend." It took a long breath. And replied, "I have been waiting my whole life for this."
>
> — Nayyirah Waheed

WORDS WILL NEVER HURT ME

The old saying "Sticks and stones may break my bones, but words will never hurt me" sounds like great wisdom, but when it comes to our bodies, what others say to us, or what we say to ourselves, can have a big-time, emotionally bruising impact. Mindfulness is wonderful because it is all about nonjudgment.

Just think about how these two words "I'm fat" or "You're fat" can produce negative thoughts and feelings about your body, and how this can lead to either healthy or unhealthy behaviors in how you treat your body.

But as you learn to notice words about your body without judgment, you will feel emotionally less triggered and less critical of yourself. As you scan the following words, reflect on each one and simply notice your thoughts and immediate impulses without judging them.

Models	Nose	Six-Pack
Skinny	Chest	Thighs
Disgusting	Heavy	Shame
Bloated	Puffy	Embarrassed
Huge	Straight Hair	Flabby
Whale	Wavy Hair	Ugly
Hot	Freckles	Gorgeous
Best Body Part	Zits	Beautiful
Worst Body Part	Pimples	Plain
Best Feature	Gross	Petite
Hairy	Attractive	Ripped
Lean	Loose	Muscular
Arms	Tight Abs	Firm

Although mindfulness won't influence how puberty changes your body during your teen years, it *will* help you to feel more at peace with your body during this period of rapid physical change. Try the following mindfulness exercise, and see how it help helps lower your body-image anxiety.

As with the other activities throughout this book, however, don't set yourself up to burn out or bail on them by forcing yourself to do them for a certain length of time or with a certain frequency. At the same time, please realize that the more you practice a given tool, the more you will get out of it.

ACCEPTING YOUR
CHANGING BODY

Take a deep breath. As you breathe in, silently tell yourself: "I feel accepting of my changing body." As you breathe out, say, "My love for my changing body is constant." Do this three times.

Now hug yourself with an intention to feel accepting of your body's changes.

Breathe in with affirming gratitude for being able to think about your body in a less judgmental way.

Now consider how it felt to view your body's changes in a more mindfully accepting way.

Can you see how acceptance of your bodily changes can help you begin to feel freer to have a more positive body image?

_____

_____

_____

What other things can you begin to enjoy more if you worry less about the way you look?

_____

_____

_____

How does being accepting of our bodies actually help us to set up even more realistic goals to improve aspects of our physical selves in a reasonable, healthy way?

_____

_____

_____

Now that we have begun trying to understand your puberty-related changes, and introduced a mindful way to relate to them, let's consider how you may worry when comparing yourself to your peers.

BEING BODY-ANXIOUS OVER MEASURING UP

You likely want to feel that you look good compared to those around you. It is easy to feel self-conscious when walking through the hallways in school. If you ever feel disappointed and upset after you negatively compare your looks to those of your peers, that does not mean there is anything wrong with you. The physical changes that you go through as a teen, combined with wanting to feel accepted by friends, makes it understandable if you worry about measuring up to the perceived attractiveness of your peers.

Even if you are not actively comparing yourself to others, comments and reactions from your friends and peers can have a lot of influence over how you feel about your own attractiveness. Friends may not realize how damaging their teasing and negative comments can be, but remarks that find fault with your appearance can be really hurtful. Even indirect, nonspecific comments such as "You look different" may feel unsettling.

Following is a tool to mindfully manage your urges to unfavorably compare your appearance to that of your peers. This is not meant as a "quick fix," but as an ongoing practice for a more positive body image. Doing this at least twice a week, for even five minutes, can really help you feel less worried about body-image issues.

SEE YOUR WORLD IN A MINDFUL WAY

When you see the world in a mindful way, you notice its beauty without making conscious comparisons. In just a few steps, you can begin to learn how to shift your thinking in this way.

1. Take a few calming, mindful breaths.

2. Imagine and reflect on a beautiful flower. Or search the web to find a picture of a flower, or situate yourself to look at a real flower.

3. Notice the flower on its own. Look at the uniqueness of its petals and how they are attached.

4. Notice the individual beauty of this flower. Yes, it may have some weeds surrounding it, yet it's pleasant to look at—there's just something about it that makes it special.

5. Now focus on a mental image of yourself surrounded by your peers.

6. Following what we discussed earlier with NOW (Notice, Observe, and be Willing), getting in touch with your value helps you feel better about yourself. Please notice your own uniqueness and beauty as you are working through this exercise. "Know your value" are three wonderful words that help you to feel good about yourself. "Know your value" is a really helpful mantra to find the "good stuff" in your appearance. If you have been struggling with a negative body image and have a hard time seeing anything uniquely beautiful about yourself, then take another look at yourself through the same eyes that you used to see the image of a flower. Cherish the color of your eyes, your smile, your hair, your dimples, your jawline, or your cheekbones just as you did the parts of the flower.

7. Notice how freeing it feels to value yourself with your "nature eyes" and not feel tied to how you look in comparison to others.

How did it feel to look at your body with "nature eyes"?

_____

Can you see how nature images can help you know your value, since you are part of nature, too?

_____

Can you see how flowers that have flaws are just as special and beautiful when you focus on them just being there without judging them or comparing them to other flowers?

_____

CBT FOR BODY-IMAGE ANXIETY

You probably have a good sense of how having a negative body image can lower your self-esteem and lead to persistent feelings of anxiety. Your body image entails a mental image of your physical body and appearance in general—its shape, size, and how it looks. Further, your body image entails your thoughts, feelings, and behaviors in response to how you see, and perceive how others see, your appearance.

The highly influential world of social media bombards you as a teen with pictures of happy people with seemingly great bodies. It's fine to have some gentle curiosity about what it would be like to have different hair or facial features or body type. But persistently engaging in negative self-talk can take you away from appreciating the body you have. "Shoulding" on yourself is one way this happens, so try the tool on the following page to overcome trashing yourself with "shoulds."

The word "should" can play a cruel role in creating anxiety over our body image. Phrases like "I should," "I need to," or "I must" all serve to be exaggerations and distortions of our perceptions of our bodies.

What is important to keep in mind is that when you "should" all over yourself you end up feeling a different "Sh"—which is "shame," as mentioned on page 36. But when you think in more flexible ways, you'll notice that your anxiety over your body image will drop considerably.

STOP "SHOULDING" ANXIETY
ON YOUR BODY

For each of the "body-image shoulds" below, try an alternative body-image thought, one that is healthier and calming, such as "would like" or "will work toward" or, best of all, "I am okay as I am." Notice that the first example includes both types of thoughts—anxiety-activating and, on the other hand, calming—to help guide you in completing this tool.

Anxiety-Inducing Body-Image Thought:

"Wow, I'm fat. I should be thinner like the other girls I see in the hallways at school."

Calming Body-Image Thought:

"I will work toward becoming healthier, but I love myself no matter how my body looks."

Anxiety-Inducing Body-Image Thought:

"I should not have any anxiety about how I look, because none of the other kids do."

Calming Body-Image Thought:

_____

Anxiety-Inducing Body-Image Thought:

"I'll never be an attractive person!"

Calming Body-Image Thought:

_____

Anxiety-Inducing Body-Image Thought:

"I'm ugly!"

Calming Body-Image Thought:

_____

Anxiety-Inducing Body-Image Thought:

"I should be happy with my body, but I can't be."

Calming Body-Image Thought:

_____

LEARNING TO
ACCEPT MY BODY

Check out the following "what if" statements and counter them with, "What if I learn to accept my body?" An example is provided to help you complete this exercise.

What if I break out with zits tomorrow when I see this guy I like in my math class?

If I say, instead, "What if I learn to accept my body?", then I realize that pressuring myself to look perfect is pointless and will just get in the way.

What if _____?

If I say, instead, "What if I learn to accept my body?", then_____.

What if _____?

If I say, instead, "What if I learn to accept my body?", then _____.

What if _____?

If I say, instead, "What if I learn to accept my body?", then _____.

What if _____?

If I say, instead, "What if I learn to accept my body?", then _____.

What if _____?

If I say, instead, "What if I learn to accept my body?", then_____.

What if _____?

If I say, instead, "What if I learn to accept my body?", then_____.

ACCEPTING YOUR BODY
WITH AFFIRMATIONS

Affirmations are positive statements that you make about yourself to feel empowered. Consistent with the philosophy of positive psychology, affirmations help you "dwell in well."

Practice saying each of the following affirmations by repeating them three times, and then ask yourself which ones resonate most with you and make you feel empowered about your body image.

- My body deserves to be taken care of.
- I am beautiful inside and out.
- Who I am is much more about loving who I am, not how I look.
- Food is the nurturer of my body, not the enemy.
- My value in this world is based on what I offer to others and not how they see me.
- I deserve to be treated with love and respect no matter how I look.
- My opinion of myself is the one that truly counts.
- Legs and hips, thanks for getting me where I want to go.
- A missing knowledge gap is worse for my life than a missing thigh gap.

Which affirmations seem most helpful to you?

_____

_____

How can saying affirmations in support of your appearance help you feel good on the inside, too?

_____

_____

What is the likely effect over time of saying body-image affirmations to yourself?

_____

_____

USING GRIT
TO GET YOUR BODY FIT

Letting your looks govern how you feel about your body can be a slippery slope to obsessing about it. But giving your body opportunities for developing grit can help you gain a healthy appreciation for it. For any fitness-related endeavors, such as those suggested in this activity, please do not overextend yourself in an unhealthy way. If you have any medical concerns, it is always best to consult a health care professional to ensure that you are in solid health to support physical challenges.

Pick one of the following fitness challenges, create a personal goal, and see how much you feel appreciation for your body as it gets stronger and performs for you.

- Do a push-up challenge. You can begin push-ups on your knees if, at first, it is too difficult to do so in the standard push-up plank position.
- Walk for a specified time or distance.
- Run for a specified time or distance.
- Do timed burpees or go for a specified number.
- Hold a plank for a specified time.

Try doing any of these challenges over two weeks.

Did you make any progress?

_____

_____

How does making progress on a physical challenge help you feel better about your physical self?

_____

_____

When you put your body to the test of a physical challenge, how does doing so take you away from thinking negatively and anxiously about it?

_____

_____

_____

BODY-IMAGE ANXIETY

In the body-images tools you've tried out so far, you have thought about yourself. Now, see if you can help Erica with *her* body-image anxiety. The more you help Erica, the more you will be helping yourself, too.

Erica finds herself in the following situation:

She is supposed to go to a dance with her friends. But the dress that Erica wanted to wear no longer fits. Plus, making matters worse, she just discovered a huge pimple on her forehead. Now she feels disgusted. She really wants to skip the dance and just message her friends that she feels sick.

Put a check mark next to each way Erica can experience a sense of flow in order to take a break from her anxiety and help herself go to the dance.

____ Write a poem about what going to the dance might mean to her.

____ Draw a picture of all the cool things she could experience at the dance.

____ Dance to one of her favorite jams in her room, while striving for flow.

____ Let the magic of the music lift her mood as she dances in her room.

____ Visualize herself dancing at the dance itself and feeling the beat of the music.

____ Visualize herself at the dance laughing while hanging with friends she trusts and feels safe with.

How can focusing while in a state of flow help Erica get out of ruminating about her body image?

_____

_____

What does flow provide Erica in terms of expanding her awareness of what feels good about who she is beyond just how she looks?

_____

_____

What can you learn from Erica and apply to yourself for putting flow in your own life to move past body-image anxiety?

_____

_____

MINDFULNESS FOR FAMILY-RELATED ANXIETY

Anxiety comes into play when we're around family because we feel uncertain about when certain pressures, struggles, and conflicts might emerge. It's common to feel stress from the anxiety of not knowing how to cope with family members when you see things differently. As a teen, you are forming your own views about what works best for you. But your parents have known you all your life, and they may have different priorities in mind when it comes to what you want to do at school, with friends, and at home. Let's look at how to use mindfulness to lower your angst at home with family.

FINDING PEACE
WITH YOUR PARENTS

When you're feeling upset about things going on in your family, you can call on mindfulness to calm yourself.

Take a few mindful breaths.

1. Focus your mind on your parents' love and caring intentions for you.

2. Breathe in, reflecting without judgment on their loving concern for you.

3. Breathe out any negative thoughts and feelings you have toward them for what they have done in the past or what they are doing now that bothers you.

4. Breathe in again, reflecting without judgment on their loving concern for you.

5. Breathe out, sending them peaceful feelings and gratitude for caring about you.

Repeat these steps in order, three times.

Now try to reflect on what it was like to slow down and not just think about your parents in a reactive way.

Were you more able to see things from their point of view?

_____

_____

_____

What are some ways that being less reactive with your emotions might actually result in you having less intense and fewer conflicts—and how this might lower anxiety in these situations?

_____

_____

_____

Can you see how understanding their point of view can keep you feeling calmer when you express yourself to them?

_____

_____

_____

SENDING CALMING ENERGY
TO SIBLINGS

Do you find that your siblings create uncertainty and anxiety in your life? Maybe you need to be somewhere and you're concerned they'll hog the shower and make you late. Perhaps you're worried that your siblings' behavior could leave you feeling embarrassed. Maybe you believe that your sibling relationships should have more harmony, and you feel anxious that it just isn't so.

Focusing on mindful feelings of positive intention toward your siblings can lower the anxiety that results from how they act with you and around you. It will help you resist the urge to keep score, and it will leave you feeling less stressed out.

Here is an exercise to help you feel less stressed out with your sibs. This activity can be practiced before typical triggering situations with a sibling, such as the examples shown below in step 1. Try practicing this exercise whenever you feel really frustrated or have other negative feelings about your siblings, such as before you go to bed or in the morning right before you actually see them.

1. Reflect on what you struggle about with your sibling(s). For example, maybe your older brother has a super-loud voice or stomps around as if he has lead feet. Or maybe your sister seems to live in the bathroom, or goes crazy on the toilet paper or shampoo, leaving none for you. Or how about those cereal-slurping younger sibs who drive you up the wall amid the morning madness?
2. Breathe in positive intention for a better sibling relationship.
3. Breathe out while visualizing your sibling frustrations as giant floats passing by in a parade.
4. Breathe in caring for a calmer, more connected sibling relationship.
5. Breathe out, visualizing each of your frustrations disappearing on the floats as the parade marches away into the distance.

Repeat steps one through five, three times.

What was it like to release anxiety toward your sibling(s) with this visualization?

_____

_____

How do you think your siblings will likely feel and respond to you if you are calmer, more accepting, and less anxious in response to them?

_____

_____

FAMILY LOSS AND ANXIETY

Families can experience all kinds of changes and losses. This can include divorce and loss of a loved one. Any kind of loss that creates major changes can lead to big-time anxiety. I have seen some divorces that are turbulent and others that involved relatively smooth transitions. Some divorcing parents support one another through healthy co-parenting, which helps their children adjust to their new lives. Even amid significant divorce-related stress, some teens seem better able than others to negotiate not only the normal challenges that arise when a family goes through divorce but also sudden, unforeseen challenges. The same varied coping and adjustment applies to the loss of a loved one as well.

If you are in a divorce situation or you know someone that is, it's common to want to prevent parents from divorcing. Sometimes there may be self-imposed blame on the part of children and teens, who may feel, irrationally, as if the divorce is their fault. Others have high anxiety because they often end up in the middle of conflicts between their parents, where they struggle to keep both parents happy. They may feel pressure to "side" with one parent and to trash-talk, lie about, or even spy on the other. In many cases, teens have expressed to me that going back and forth between two homes is stressful in itself. And I often hear about blended family issues, too.

The following exercise, while mainly about divorce, can also provide comfort if you have experienced the loss of a loved one in your life.

The acronym RAIN, first coined about twenty years ago by Michele McDonald, is an easy-to-remember tool for practicing mindfulness. RAIN stands for *recognizing* feelings, *allowing* them to be present, *investigating* what these feelings mean, and *not judging* or defining yourself about these feelings. In the following tool, RAIN will be broken into steps like this:

R: Recognize

A: Allow

I: Inquire and investigate

N: Not totally defining yourself (the tool will clarify)

Now let's use RAIN for dealing with sadness related to divorce.

WASH AWAY FAMILY LOSS

RAIN can be used for mindfulness in many ways. In the steps below, let's apply it to letting go of pain related to divorce.

Breathe in and out mindfully a few times. Then step into the RAIN:

R: Recognize the thoughts and feelings you have related to your parents' divorce. Are they mostly negative, or are there some positive ones, too, such as realizing that you don't have to hear your parents quarreling under the same roof anymore, or having some new opportunities for alone time with each of your parents?

A: Allow those feelings to be present. Don't try to fight or suppress them, but accept them as they are.

I: Inquire and investigate how these thoughts and feelings have shaped the way you experience your parents' divorce. Has the divorce created changes that are hard to accept? Have any of the transitions due to the divorce been easier than you thought they would be?

N: Not totally defining yourself: Ask yourself: "Do these thoughts and feelings about my parents' divorce have to define me, or can they just be part of me? Are there empowering ways to define myself apart from my parents' divorce?" It may, for example, feel good to reflect on your love for each of your parents, realizing that you may express it differently to each one. Or perhaps you can think about your extended family on either or both sides being consistently in your life, as a way to strengthen your sense of family and ease any negative feelings from changes in your immediate family. You can also remind yourself that even though your parents are divorced, you still, and will always be, a family. Be mindful, as well, that you are not alone: many other kids have survived and thrived even though their parents divorced.

How did it feel to notice your parents' divorce in a mindful way by being in the RAIN?

_____

_____

How can mindfully reflecting on their divorce (or any kind of loss in your family) help you see it in a less anxious way?

_____

_____

SEEING THE EVIDENCE FOR
DISTORTED THOUGHTS

Just like a prosecutor in a courtroom, your distorted thoughts from your reactive brain try to make a case to create and justify your family-related anxiety. Knowing how your mind creates "evidence" by thinking a certain way can help you begin to deal with your anxiety.

Take a few moments to notice the types of thoughts, feelings, and behaviors that relate to your anxious feelings about family members in stressful situations you face with them. Now ask yourself about the evidence for seeing these thoughts, feelings, and behaviors as you currently do. Use the following questions to guide you through this process.

What are some behaviors of certain family members that trigger you to feel anxious?

_____

_____

_____

What unreasonable and maybe even extreme thoughts do you sometimes have about certain family members, and what is the evidence to truly support the truth of these thoughts?

_____

_____

_____

How do your counterproductive thoughts build even more "evidence" (which becomes even more distorted as you get more and more upset) that gets in the way of connecting and feeling closer to these family members?

_____

_____

_____

Can you see how your "evidence" for your thoughts, when faulty, blocks you from feeling calmer around certain family members?

_____

_____

_____

DISPUTING ANXIOUS
THOUGHTS ABOUT FAMILY

One way to throw out faulty evidence is to dispute it. Please put a check mark below in front of any of the potentially more helpful ways to reframe, which helps you dispute your upsetting thoughts about family members:

_____ "She is lazy." vs. "She struggles at times with motivation."

_____ "He has to be right." vs. "He feels passionate."

_____ "She's a bitch." vs. "She is likely hurting inside."

_____ "He's messed up." vs. "He is probably confused."

_____ "He's a slob." vs. "He has a hard time getting organized."

_____ "He is a problem." vs. "His limitations create problems."

_____ "She ruins this family." vs. "She creates challenges but they can provide life lessons."

_____ "You can't talk to him." vs. "Maybe my approach is not working and there is a better one."

_____ "I hate it here." vs. "The more I learn to accept what I can't change about this aspect of my family, the more I can learn to cope with it."

What are the benefits of reframing your counterproductive beliefs about family members?

_____

_____

How can reframing your negative thoughts about them lower your anxiety?

_____

_____

How can reframing these thoughts also create new opportunities to understand and get along with family members?

_____

_____

TAKING ACTION TO
LOWER FAMILY ANXIETY

CBT is all about changing your thoughts, feelings, and behaviors. Sometimes directly changing your behaviors—including when it comes to what you do with family members who influence you to feel anxious—can help you think, feel, and be in a better place with them.

Put a check mark next to some positive steps you can take, together with family members, to lower your negative energy with them.

____ Go for a walk.

____ Play a board game.

____ Watch a show or movie.

____ Go bowling.

____ Play a video game.

____ Cowrite a story.

____ Make paper airplanes.

____ Do crafts.

____ Write a song.

____ Cook a meal.

____ Go for a bike ride.

____ Create a family tree.

____ Start a collection of rocks, coins, etc.

____ Work on a jigsaw puzzle.

____ Play tic-tac-toe or hangman.

____ Create a scrapbook.

____ Do yardwork.

____ Create a movie with family pictures.

____ Do a collaborative drawing on a sheet of poster board.

____ Take turns reading aloud.

____ Look at the clouds or stars and share what the shapes mean to each person.

What thoughts and feelings do you have when you look at the actionable new possibilities of spending time together with family members?

_____

_____

_____

How can changing how you spend time together change some dynamics in your family?

_____

_____

_____

How can changing what you do with family members lower your anxiety for when you anticipate being around them?

_____

_____

_____

Why do we resist getting out of our comfort zones and not initiating new ways to interact with family members?

_____

_____

_____

FEELING IN TOUCH
WITH FAMILY STRENGTHS

When you feel anxiety over family issues, discovering what matters in terms of what you value about your family can help lower your concerns. Take a few minutes to visualize each of your family members and your family as a whole. While doing so, reflect on the following questions.

What are some strengths of your parents and/or siblings that you admire?

_____

_____

_____

How does valuing their strengths help you feel less stressed out when you're around them?

_____

_____

_____

How would your family members respond to your sharing how much you value their strengths?

_____

_____

_____

What, if anything, holds you back from sharing with them how much you value their strengths?

_____

_____

_____

LOSING FAMILY ANXIETY
BY GAINING GRATITUDE

Gratitude plays a valuable role in helping you to see, in a positive way, the role that each of your family members plays in your life. Take a few minutes to reflect on these gratitude-related questions to help you connect to what you appreciate about your family.

What are three things you are grateful for in your family?

_____

_____

_____

Ask each family member to take turns (or imagine them doing so) writing down what they would name as things to be grateful for. If family members are resistant to doing this, then simply try to take their perspectives and imagine what you think they think and feel about gratitude.

How does focusing on gratitude for and within your family help you lower anxious feelings when you're around them?

_____

_____

_____

What have you learned about gratitude that could help your family?

_____

_____

_____

FLOWING OUT OF
ANXIETY WITH FAMILY

Flow is the emotional state you experience when you are on a roll and super engaged when doing a favorite activity. The more you get absorbed in flow with a family member or in a family activity, the less anxiety you will be aware of at that time.

Check out the list of activities you saw earlier under the tool called "Taking Action to Lower Family Anxiety" (page 90). Pick one of those activities to do with a family member with whom you have had some struggles. Be gentle in your request, ensuring that this family member will be comfortable with the time and place of your suggested activity. If the family member seems reluctant, go for an activity of shorter duration and express appreciation for her or his willingness to engage in this with you.

Notice what happens to your sense of time as you do something together that you are both immersed in. Does time seem to fly by more quickly when doing something together that you both enjoy?

_____

_____

What is your shared motivation level for spending time together doing an activity that you both feel absorbed in?

_____

_____

How does flow change your focus from externally noticing things you find challenging about your family member(s) to internally feeling a sense of connection by working together toward a shared goal?

_____

_____

What does it feel like to connect in new ways with family members whom you had felt disconnected from?

_____

_____

_____

How can flow help you lower your anxiety toward family issues?

_____

_____

_____

Part B | COPING WITH DEPRESSION

GETTING TO KNOW DEPRESSION

Often the terms *sadness* and *depression* are used interchangeably. Have you ever been sad over disappointments or losses such as a bad grade? Have you experienced peer issues such as feeling like you don't connect or enduring a difficult breakup? Have you struggled with a family problem, or suffered the loss of a loved one?

Maybe you have felt sad at times about such concerns. Sadness is a temporary state. When it is more persistent, however, then it can often be seen as depression.

Depression, like sadness, consists of negative, pessimistic thoughts—but of a more intense nature than typical feelings of sadness. Depression runs in families and is the result of both genetics and stressful events. *Sadness* and *depression* overlap, but depression is more severe.

There are different levels of depression. A more moderate form of depression is called *dysthymia*. When depression becomes more severe, it can progress to the point that people are unable to function or feel suicidal. With major depression, people likely find it difficult to perform simple daily tasks, feel hopeless and helpless, and lose interest in the things they used to like to do. Some people have bipolar disorder, which means alternating between manic feelings (racing thoughts and intense yearnings toward unrealistic goals) and very down periods of profound hopelessness.

Given that you and your peers can vary greatly in terms of what are referred to as feelings of sadness vs. actual depression, to avoid confusion and to promote variety in word usage, the terms *sadness* and *depression* will be used interchangeably in this workbook.

The common symptoms of depression in teens include both emotional signs and behavioral signs.

Emotional signs of depression:
- You have persistent sad feelings, possibly including crying spells, that may or may not be related to current concerns.
- You feel hopeless or empty.
- You're touchy, showing frustration or feelings of anger even about little things.
- You're more irritable in general.
- You feel that nothing seems fun anymore—even activities you have really liked to do in the past—and you just don't see value in pushing yourself to do them.
- You've been withdrawing from family and friends and have increased conflicts with them.
- You have strong feelings of worthlessness or guilt.
- You have been dwelling on past failures or attacking yourself with blame or criticism.
- You realize that paying attention and focusing are challenging for you.
- You struggle with making decisions and remembering things.
- You are super sensitive to rejection or failure, and you need excessive reassurance.

- You see your future in a bleak, negative way.
- You have increased thoughts of death, dying, or suicide.

Behavioral signs of depression:
- You have a hard time falling asleep or are sleeping too much.
- You feel more tired than usual and have a loss of energy.
- You have decreased appetite and weight loss, or increased cravings for food and weight gain.
- You've been using alcohol or drugs to cope with feeling down in the dumps.
- You're showing signs of agitation or restlessness—for example, pacing, hand-wringing, or an inability to sit still.
- Your mind feels foggy with slowed thinking, and speaking feels more challenging.
- You have unexplained body aches and headaches.
- You've been isolating yourself from others.
- Your school performance has dipped or you've had frequent absences from school.
- It seems harder to take care of your personal hygiene or appearance.
- You've had some angry outbursts, disruptive or risky behavior, or other acting-out behaviors.
- You've engaged in self-harm—for example, cutting, burning, or excessive piercing or tattooing.
- You're considering making a suicide plan or a suicide attempt.

If You Have Suicidal Thoughts

Passive thoughts of wondering what it would be like if you were no longer alive are not easy to go through, but they are fairly common. If, however, you're feeling like there is no other way to cope than harming yourself or others, or taking your life or that of others, you need to get help right now. It takes guts to even consider getting some support when feeling suicidal. When it feels like the walls are closing in, you can use that courage to help you keep going and overcome depression.

Whether you seek out a friend, family member, teacher, or anyone else you can trust, it is crucial that you seek help. If you feel there is no one to talk to, then please call the national suicide prevention lifeline at 1-800-273-TALK (8255). You'll be able to speak confidentially to someone who understands what you're going through and can help you deal with your feelings.

Depression is a general term that you have likely heard referred to, and perhaps have personally considered, in many ways. Now let's explore your own ideas about depression with the following tool.

DEPRESSION

BY OTHER NAMES

Consider each of the following words and phrases that people may use to describe feeling depressed. Please circle any that seem to resonate with how you feel when you are sad or depressed.

Hopeless	Nothing	Ineffective
Inferior	Worthless	Helpless
Less Than	Empty	Left Behind
Rejected	Hollow	I'm Used to It
Lonely	Inadequate	Nothing Matters
Aimless	Dark	Meaningless

Which of these words best describe how you feel when you are depressed?

_____

_____

_____

Which of the negative words above do you hear your peers say (or see them appear to feel) when they express that they are feeling sad or depressed?

_____

_____

_____

Which words from the above list would you *not* typically use to describe your emotions when feeling depressed? Why?

_____

_____

_____

WHAT ARE YOUR
TRIGGERS OF SADNESS?

Many types of situations can trigger or worsen depressed feelings. Reflect on the possible causes of your depressed thoughts and feelings when you experience them. Then put a circle around any of the situations below that lead you to feel sad or possibly depressed at times:

Left Out of Plans

Negative Comments on Social Media

Relationship breakup

Parents Fighting

Divorce

Disconnected Friends

Loss of a Relative

Witnessing Others Struggling

Physical Illness

Family Tensions at Home

Changing Financial Circumstances

Poor Grades

Not Making a Team

Upsetting Event at a Job

Conflict with a Teacher

Body-Image Issues

Feeling like You Don't Fit In

Burned Out from School

Being Bullied

How can being more aware of these situations help to minimize future sad feelings about them?

_____

_____

How does holding in your feelings about these situations lead you to feel sad or depressed?

_____

_____

Who have you talked to, or who could you talk to, about these concerns?

_____

_____

How might you comfort a friend who has these concerns?

_____

_____

Just as those struggling with anxiety often feel shame about it, many teens relate to depression in a similar way—like there is something disgraceful about feeling sad. You may keep your depressed thoughts and feelings to yourself because you believe that your depression is a downer or that it embarrasses you.

If you feel that school hallways are like the runways in a fashion show, or that social media creates images of perfect lives, then you are likely putting a lot of pressure on yourself, especially if you think that hurting inside means there is something wrong with you. You may recall how we discussed the pressure to look like everything is FINE, as discussed back in the section called "When 'FINE' Appearances May Be Deceiving" (page 62).

UNCOVERING SHAME
AROUND DEPRESSION

Let's look at some common negative terms perceived by those who shame themselves for struggling with depression. By identifying these shame-related depression descriptors in the tool below, you can then be on the lookout to make sure you don't get sucked into them as well.

Notice the shame words relating to depression below. Circle any of these negative, shaming associations that you may at times relate to when you are concerned about what others may think if they know you feel depressed.

Draining	Too Deep	Oversensitive
Weak	Too Serious	Pathetic
Defective	Heavy	Contagious
Dark	Loner	Loser
Less Than	Not Fitting In	Babyish
No Fun	Psycho	Screwed Up

Which, if any, of the above negative terms have you ever associated with depression?

_____

_____

_____

Which of these terms have you heard your peers use to refer to themselves or others who are facing challenges related to depression?

_____

_____

_____

Why do you think people tend to see depression in a negative way?

_____

_____

_____

How can depression be made worse by seeing it in a negative way vs. something you can work on and overcome?

_____

_____

_____

To further explore the situations that lead you to see your depressed feelings in negative ways, complete the following statement:

When I get depressed, I tend to beat myself up by saying this to myself:

_____

_____

_____

THE COST OF COVERING UP DEPRESSION

You can make yourself more vulnerable to problematically managing your depressed thoughts and feelings by silently suffering and shutting down from others. I refer to this as becoming "emotionally constipated." Ugh! Although this term may initially sound amusing and maybe even revolting, holding in your negative, upset feelings can become a big problem, paving the way for depression to keep creeping in and remaining internalized, or stuck within you. Often, holding in depressed feelings involves denying that they exist within yourself, or denying them to others.

GETTING OUT OF
DENIAL RIVER

Let's look at a situation with Beth, who denied her depressed feelings about an important school project. See how you might help her out in the tool below.

Beth received a disappointing grade on an English paper and acted detached when her parents asked her about it. Her parents thought she really did not care, even though she did. Reflect on the following questions about her situation.

What are some possible reasons Beth may have chosen to act like she did not care when she received this bad grade?

_____
_____
_____

What would be a better, healthier way for her to respond to her parents?

_____
_____
_____

How can denying sad situations lead to more significant depression?

_____
_____
_____

What are some other feelings that may accompany sadness in Beth's situation?

_____
_____
_____

How could Beth have felt better by opening up to her concerned parents about her disappointment and her sad feelings?

_____
_____

MORE UNHEALTHY WAYS TO DEAL WITH DEPRESSION

Here are some further examples of unhealthy ways that teens may manage their depressed feelings, ways that don't turn out so well. If you have tried some of these, you are certainly not alone—we're all human, and depression (or any upsetting emotions such as anxiety or anger) can lead us to cope in some of the following unhealthy ways.

Withdrawing and Avoiding Behaviors

As a teen you likely just want to feel normal and not sad or depressed. It is common to have anxiety about your anxiety, and you can also be depressed over feeling depressed. Where this mostly manifests itself is in withdrawing or avoiding others, which then feeds on itself, leading to more of the same.

Sometimes it may feel tempting to turn away from your demands and responsibilities. But this can rob you of valuable opportunities to help yourself feel less depressed. For example, if you lack confidence and so you avoid starting a conversation with the person you like because it makes you uncomfortable, then you won't get to know them. As a result, you may feel sad or empty because you're missing out on a really cool connection you might have with that person.

Overeating or Undereating

As you have learned so far, upsetting, stressful thoughts lead to upsetting emotions and reactions felt in your body. One unfortunately common way that people cope with depressed feelings is by eating—too much and too often. This is often referred to as *emotional eating*, where people try to soothe sadness and emotional emptiness with food. Another way that some depressed people cope is by not eating enough, which can be even more destructive.

For persistent or worsening problematic eating, please talk with your parents or some other caring adult in your life about seeing a qualified mental health professional.

Coping with Drugs or Alcohol or Self-Harm/Reckless Behaviors

Sadly many teens (and adults) turn to unhealthy ways to fill the void that depression leaves in their lives. Maybe you or teens you know have tried drinking alcohol or smoking marijuana and using other drugs to escape from feeling down. Often it can be hard to clearly see how drug use is frequently connected to underlying depression. Whether seemingly innocent curiosity leads to experimentation with drugs or not, people may use drugs to self-medicate their sadness (or anxiety or anger). This, however, may lead to more problems, including harming your body and creating addictions. Engaging in self-harming behaviors such as cutting is another unhealthy way of escaping sadness. And if you or someone you know feels suicidal, it is essential to see a qualified mental health professional immediately.

Excessive Screen Time

Using screen time as an escape from sadness and depression may not seem like a significant concern to some teens. Yet the allure of social media, television shows, and video games can really become a problem when these digital distractions keep you from meeting demands and facing pressures in your life. For most teens, simply acknowledging how captivating screen time can be is an important step in setting and sticking to reasonable time limits.

At the same time, it's not always easy to follow through on the intention to reduce screen-time distractions. It can be very appealing to binge-watch shows or let one level of a video game suck you into another one.

An important consideration in determining whether you need to cut back on screen time is to look at how you spend your time overall. Do you participate in activities such as sports, the arts, clubs at school, or a part-time job? Is your screen use interfering with your ability to get an adequate amount of sleep? Compromised sleep can worsen your depressed feelings.

Many mobile devices have apps that can track your screen time. Would you be able to have a collaborative and mutually supportive working goal with your parents to keep each other accountable for keeping family screen-time use within an acceptable range? Would putting your phone or other mobile device out of sight for the night help you get better sleep? Drawing from these ideas or having some other kind of self-monitoring method in place can really help you to avoid getting lost in screens.

If you have ever coped with depression in unproductive or even destructive ways, please don't be hard on yourself. In reading these pages, you have come a long way in learning how to deal with depression. And it may also help you to look at how you are not alone in this struggle.

YOU ARE NOT ALONE

Because people may try to cover feelings of depression, it is easy to believe—falsely—that you are the only one suffering from it. Broaden your awareness of how many others struggle by completing the questions below.

What do you observe in other people who feel depressed?

_____

_____

_____

What do people say when they feel depressed?

_____

_____

_____

In the following list, circle the moods and behaviors that are commonly shown by people who are depressed:

Isolated	Using Drugs	Withdrawn
Irritable	Crying	Quiet
Tired	Self-Harming	Disengaged
Overeating	Sensitive	Lethargic
Not Eating	Angry	Preoccupied

How do you or others try to hide these behaviors?

_____

_____

_____

LEARNING BEST
IN THE PRESENT MOMENT

One hugely important lesson to learn is that depression gets in the way of functioning at school. When you are struggling with feelings of depression, you will likely find it harder to pay attention and focus on what is being taught in class.

Check out the table below, which shows how using mindfulness for school-related depression can really help you feel less weighed down and more tuned in.

Sadness at School Drives You to Be . . .	Mindfulness Gently Guides You to Be . . .
caught up and self-critical in your own thoughts.	tuned in to school demands with awareness.
negative, with a closed attitude.	curious and open in your attitude to being more willing to learn.
inflexible and struggling with your attention, narrowly focused.	flexible with your attention, and more aware of what's going on around you.
dismissive and uncaring.	more aware of the value of doing things to help yourself learn and grow.

What are some sad thoughts that you get caught up in at school?

_____

_____

How do these thoughts take you away from being in the present moment?

_____

_____

How can tuning in to the present moment help you connect more in class, with peers, and in school-related activities?

_____

_____

How does being in the present moment at school help you overcome feelings of depression that can otherwise leave you internally preoccupied and less able to learn?

_____

_____

RESET YOUR MOOD
WITH BREATHING

When you feel like you've lost track of what is going on at school, you can feel reassured by just knowing that you can always find your breath. Noticing your breath is a great way to get re-centered when sad feelings are getting the best of you.

Simply find a quiet place and sit comfortably. Once you're settled, if it feels right to you, let your eyes gently close. Or you can gaze softly at a spot a few feet in front of you, looking at nothing in particular.

1. Focus your attention on your breath.
2. As you breathe in, say to yourself, "I'm breathing in knowledge."
3. Pay attention to the sensations of your breath passing into your body.
4. As you breathe out, say to yourself, "I'm breathing out boredom and resistance to learning new things."
5. Observe the sensations in your body related to your out breath.
6. Notice whether your attention is on your breath, or whether it has wandered to thoughts about other things.
7. Continue to gently maintain your awareness on (or return your awareness to) your breath.
8. Repeat steps 1–7 three or four times.

Can you see how mindful breathing offers you a soothing way to re-center yourself, lift yourself up, and move away from down feelings?

_____

_____

_____

Can you see how being in the present makes you feel emotionally lighter and more prepared to learn?

_____

_____

_____

BRANCHING OUT WITH
THE BREATH EXERCISE

Sometimes sadness seems to shake us at our very roots. Here is another mindfulness activity to center yourself when feeling sad about school. It is a great activity to do in the morning before school to help set a tone of strength and confidence and to fight sad feelings. Find a quiet, comfortable space to sit comfortably and relax. Now go through the following mindfulness visualization:

Breathe in, imagining that you are connected to the ground like the roots of a tree. With each out breath, see yourself letting go of your sad feelings. Visualize a tree bending with the wind, not breaking. Now picture the gentle sun flowing into your leaves, like knowledge you are prepared to absorb today. Gently try to hold that image in your mind for about a minute. As you think of this strong yet flexible tree, accept whatever thoughts, sensations, or emotions blow your way. Let them pass you by like so many molecules of air—even your worries. Repeat this exercise one or two more times if you want to.

How did it feel to draw upon the strength and flexibility of the tree while doing your breathing?

_____

_____

Were you able to feel more sensations in your breath or body as you identified yourself with the tree image?

_____

_____

Did visualizing the tree give you a sense of strength or confidence?

_____

_____

Can visualizing the leaves and branches inspire you to extend yourself to receive important knowledge that surrounds you at school?

_____

_____

LIGHTEN YOUR LOAD
BY SMILING

Some people mistakenly view mindfulness as having to be a heavy, deep-thinking experience. By learning to be in the present with mindfulness, however, you actually feel lighter.

Think of something about your school life that you associate with negativity and sadness (e.g., tests, a specific teacher, being called on, or hard projects). Now go through the following activity:

Smile as you reflect on your concern.

Gently redirect your focus to three mindful breaths.

Now go back to the same topic, but this time frown.

Return now to your smile—keep going, as wide as you can!

Now say to yourself: "Ha ha ha, he he he, ho ho ho!"

Did this activity distract you from your school-related sad feelings?

_____

_____

_____

How did it feel to infuse yourself with smiling energy when thinking about school concerns?

_____

_____

_____

Consider putting a sticky note or some kind of sign in your room in a place where you can see it each morning as you get ready for school. As silly as this sounds, write on it the following message: "Ha ha ha, he he he, ho ho ho—off to school I go!" Repeat these words either silently or aloud to lighten your mood as you begin your day.

Staying in the present moment, repeat this message to yourself three times before going to school, and see if it helps you feel happier. (Just don't get carried away and repeat this out loud on the bus or in homeroom class! Then again, if you do, you may find you're not the only one smiling!)

CONNECTING WITH
KINDNESS AT SCHOOL

Even though some days you may feel it's debatable, you learn many great lessons at school. Here is an activity to learn how to reflect on others in order to feel better within yourself.

Think of someone or a few people at school to whom you can give a compliment. Write down what you'd say and how you'd feel.

_____

_____

_____

Visualize their talents: things like their intelligence or athletic, musical, or artistic abilities. Reflect on how these positive attributes of others help you feel happiness and admiration for them.

_____

_____

_____

Think of someone's positive personality qualities such as a sense of humor, work ethic, or kindness. Jot them down here.

_____

_____

_____

Send best wishes to someone whom you admire from afar because you don't know them very well.

_____

_____

_____

Now send positive energy and kindness to someone you don't like so much.

_____

_____

_____

What did you learn about yourself by extending kindness to others?

_____

_____

_____

How can sending out an intention of kindness for others at school help you feel better about being there too?

_____

_____

_____

CBT FOR DEPRESSED FEELINGS AT SCHOOL

Let's look at how cognitive behavioral therapy can help you identify and overcome sad feelings related to school, Here's an example:

Thought: "I have no energy to start this language arts project because I'll probably end up getting a bad grade on it, just like last time."

Feeling: Discouraged

Behavior: Procrastination toward the project

As you recall from when we discussed anxiety earlier in the book, the connection of thoughts, feelings, and behaviors is best thought of as being cyclical, as shown in this graphic:

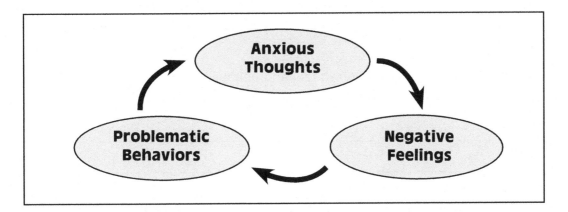

Please refer to the earlier section, "Common Distorted Thoughts Among Teens" (page 36), which describes unreasonable and counterproductive thoughts. As you may recall, CBT is about:

- identifying your unhelpful thoughts.
- questioning these distorted, problematic beliefs to see whether they are, in fact, true.
- replacing your negative, unhelpful thoughts with more positive ones.
- visualizing and carrying out emotionally healthier behaviors and making better choices about reacting to seemingly negative situations.

IDENTIFYING AND CHALLENGING
SAD SCHOOL THOUGHTS

Once you go through the steps below, you'll likely emerge with a heightened awareness of how distorted thinking weighs on you and leads to depressed feelings. Learning to identify these unhelpful thoughts gives you the ability to question and challenge them with healthier beliefs in order to stop them from getting in your way.

Think of a school-related problem you had in the past few months. Consider where you were at the time and what had happened. Just take a few minutes and reflect on this past situation.

How did thinking this way lead you to feel and behave?

_____

_____

_____

What did you say to yourself about the problem that made it feel worse?

_____

_____

_____

Put a check mark next to any of the following sadness-related feelings you were experiencing at the time:

_____ Disappointed	_____ Discouraged	_____ Disempowered
_____ Hopeless	_____ Scared	_____ Overwhelmed
_____ Filled With Doubt	_____ Hesitant	_____ Defeated
_____ Pessimistic	_____ Giving Up	_____ Upset

What is a better way to think about this situation to help you feel better?

_____

_____

_____

GETTING IT DONE
WHEN YOU FEEL DOWN

Sad, depressing thoughts can make it really hard to get your schoolwork done. Yet when you don't accomplish these and other demands, you can end up feeling even more depressed. Challenge each of the following counterproductive, hopelessness-generating thoughts with more positive, action-focused ones. The first hopeless thought and its alternative positive thought is provided for you as an example to use throughout the exercise.

Hopeless Thought

"I keep trying to start this paper but just can't do it. I'm doomed." (catastrophic conclusion)

Empowering Thought

"Just because I am having a hard time starting does not mean that I can't do a good job on this paper. Starting it now will end my feeling of being stuck."

· · · · · · · · · · · · · · · · · ·

Hopeless Thought

"Everyone else is going to do so much better than I will on this." (unfavorable comparison)

Empowering Thought

_____

Hopeless Thought

"I just can't get anything done." (all-or-nothing thinking)

Empowering Thought

_____

Hopeless Thought

"I'm stupid and will never amount to anything." (negative labeling and catastrophic thinking)

Empowering Thought

_____

MOTIVATIONALLY CONSTIPATED

You may be thinking that these tools may not be helpful because even if you can change your thoughts and mood to feeling less depressed, you may still struggle to get yourself into action mode. I want to introduce a new term, "motivationally constipated," for those times when you feel your motivation is blocked. The best way to free yourself up from a bout of motivational constipation is to get things moving by doing something. Otherwise, the more you stay stuck doing nothing, the more depressed you can end up feeling. So now let's look at some concrete behaviors that you can throw in along with thinking and feeling better to get you on the path to being more productive.

LOOKING PAST SADNESS TO
FIND SCHOOL MOTIVATION

Pushing through your motivational blocks will help you feel less depressed and ready to re-engage in school tasks. Let's look at how even doing tasks unrelated to school can prime your motivational pump and get it going.

The following is a list of things you can do to jump-start your motivation. The blank lines at the end of this motivation-boosting list are an invitation for you to add some more of your own.

Make the Bed

Clean Out a Drawer

Clean Out Your Backpack

Help Someone Do Something

Work Out

Set a Small Goal

Identify a Task You Did Even Though You Did Not Want To

Feel Pride in Reading This List

Write Down the Lyrics to a Song You Like

Watch an Inspiring Video Clip

Wash a Car

Help Someone in Your Family

Attend to the Needs of a Pet

Read a Short, Inspiring Story

Do Some Weeding or Other Form of Yard Cleanup

_____   _____

_____   _____

_____   _____

TAKE A FEEL-GOOD BREAK
FROM SCHOOL SADNESS

Engaging in an enjoyable activity helps to slow down your sad, negative school thoughts. You can take many pleasurable breaks to treat yourself to something enjoyable and calming. Some joyful activities are listed below. They can be used for time frames ranging from a minute or two to an hour or more, depending on the level of stress you are experiencing, where you are, and the time you have available to use them. Some of these you can do quickly at school to re-center yourself. You can also do them at home after school to get into homework mode, or in the morning to get into the groove for school.

Which of these breaks can you start using now to help you when you feel sad? Circle a few.

- Doodle a cool design.
- Think something positive about yourself.
- Adjust to a straighter posture.
- Draw a picture.
- Make a quick list of your past accomplishments.
- Mentally smile at someone and send it their way.
- Hug or play with your pet.
- Listen to music.
- Play a video game (just don't let this one become too frequent and too time consuming).
- Write a short story where you make up cool characters who intrigue you.
- Read a book.

What might get in the way of using feel-good breaks as a coping skill?

_____

_____

How can you overcome obstacles to using these coping strategies?

_____

_____

_____

REACHING OUT
WHEN YOU FEEL DOWN

There is a famous quotation from the English poet John Donne: "No man is an island." This means that we don't feel good when we feel alone. This is especially true when we feel depressed. Seeking support from others is helpful in reducing stress because it enables you to feel less isolated when you're facing what is bothering you. Being alone in your stress can leave you bottled up with it.

Gaining support from friends can help you avoid emotionally imploding over school stress. Reflect on someone you can text or talk to when you feel school stress. This might be a friend, family member, or someone else you trust.

Who came to mind as someone you could reach out to when you feel down?

_____

_____

How does reaching out to that person benefit them as well as you when you're facing stressful academic demands?

_____

_____

How do you feel when you help someone in need feel better about getting through school stresses?

_____

_____

What obstacle makes it hard for you to reach out for help when you feel crushed or shut down in the face of school struggles?

_____

_____

How can you overcome that obstacle?

_____

_____

POSITIVE PSYCHOLOGY FOR SCHOOL SADNESS

As you recall, part of positive psychology is learning to be optimistic. Optimism means believing that things will turn out well in the future, while pessimism refers to looking at what's ahead in a negative light.

You've likely heard the expression: "Is the glass half-empty or half-full?" This refers to being able to see stressful situations, and to hold a view of the world, in either a pessimistic or optimistic way. Pessimists are those who see the glass half-empty, and optimists see it as half-full. Pessimists tend to think more about falling short or failing in the face of challenges, while optimists see themselves conquering those same challenges.

A huge difference between pessimists and optimists is in how they think during stressful times and adversity. Pessimists tend to blame themselves when things don't go well, and they tend to see their negative circumstances in a more permanent way. For example, if you have a pessimistic view of yourself when you do poorly on a test, you might say, "I just can't learn this subject." This implies there is something wrong with you and that you just don't measure up. Thinking this way probably stresses you out because you think you have no control over the situation.

Optimists, on the other hand, are hopeful and believe they have a sense of control to make things better. So as an optimist failing a test, you'd say something like, "I'll find a better way to study this, and then I'll do better on the next test." The power of optimism is clear in a famous quote by the noted philosopher and psychologist, William James, who said, "Pessimism leads to weakness. Optimism leads to power."

Thinking optimistically calms down your reactive brain and stabilizes the amount of cortisol (a stress hormone) that is released in your body. Less cortisol means feeling less stress—which is a really good thing!

GAINING OPTIMISM

FOR SCHOOL

Do you think that some people are just born as optimists? Well, it is true that some people are more naturally wired to be optimistic than others. But what you may not realize is that becoming more optimistic is also a skill that you can learn. In fact, Martin Seligman, a noted psychologist, showed through his research that we can learn to be more optimistic by training ourselves to do so!

To begin helping you get in touch with optimism, though, let's consider the impact of pessimism (the opposite of optimism) by reflecting on the following questions.

What has it been like to experience negative energy about school coming from yourself or others?

_____

_____

_____

How do your peers complain counterproductively about the pressures that come from their schoolwork?

_____

_____

_____

Do you, too, ever complain about school struggles to your peers, maybe because all the complaining around you feels infectious? If so, how?

_____

_____

_____

Can you see how focusing on negative energy, whether within or around you, stresses you out for school? If yes, in what ways?

_____

_____

_____

Do you notice yourself feeling more upbeat about school when you expect that good things are going to happen?

_____

_____

_____

Can you see how this upbeat feeling sharply contrasts with how you feel when you think bad things are coming your way?

_____

_____

_____

How about your friends' outlooks—would you rather hang out with your friends if they're being super gloom and doom or if they are feeling more upbeat and hopeful?

_____

_____

_____

FLIPPING SCHOOL
TO THE UPSIDE

Reflect on a current school situation that you don't believe will turn out as well as you'd like it to. Think of your beliefs, feelings, and even bodily reactions as you're seeing this situation in a negative light. As you consider this situation, ask yourself the following questions:

What internal messages from my past or from others are leading to my pessimistic view of this situation?

_____

_____

Why else have I been conning myself into thinking that this not going as well as I would like?

_____

_____

What would it actually take for this experience to go well for me?

_____

_____

What unique strengths and values do I have that I can use to increase the chances of this turning out well?

_____

_____

How does thinking more optimistically change my view of this situation for the better?

_____

_____

How does thinking in a more optimistic manner spur me to take positive actions?

_____

_____

MAKE IT YOUR BEST
SCHOOL PERFORMANCE

Imagine how letting go of catastrophic thoughts about schoolwork outcomes can leave you feeling better. Now picture being successful in school while becoming less stressed about it, and reflect on the following questions:

What have you done, and what are you doing that can help you think more positively about your schoolwork?

_____

_____

_____

How does focusing on your past school success help to create a more positive mood in the present?

_____

_____

_____

In what ways does focusing on past successes and future positive school-performance outcomes inspire you to take some actions to achieve what you are visualizing?

_____

_____

_____

How does focusing on your future grades positively help you feel less stressed about them at the current time?

_____

_____

_____

ACHIEVING MORE
WITH GRIT

Think of an immediate goal for school and how achieving it will be fulfilling. Focus on a class in which you want to do better.

If you've not worked up to your potential in this class, why is that so?

_____

_____

What is a new goal you have for this class?

_____

_____

What steps do you need to take to realize this goal?

_____

_____

How will you persevere in the face of setbacks in reaching this goal?

_____

_____

How could improving in this class help you improve other parts of your life?

_____

_____

How does strengthening your grit help you get past feelings of sadness about school?

_____

_____

MELTING SCHOOL SADNESS
WITH GRATITUDE

Reflect on some teachers, friends, peers, and events that you feel pleased about regarding school.

What teachers are you grateful for?

_____

_____

What friends are you grateful for?

_____

_____

What activities are you involved in that bring you a sense of gratitude?

_____

_____

What is something your friends appreciate about you?

_____

_____

How does focusing on what you are grateful for at school help you feel less sad when you are there?

_____

_____

What do you think the future at school holds for you that you will feel grateful for?

_____

_____

DISCOVERING
SOCIAL HAPPINESS

When it comes to the social realm, it's easy to get caught up in the negative energy of drama and negative comparisons, which can leave you feeling empty and sad. Learning to become socially content through mindfulness can help prevent depressed feelings over social situations.

This activity can be applied to any interactions with others where you are looking to feel connected. By looking within yourself with a beginner's mind, you can explore how to feel more fulfilled in social interactions.

Imagine a gathering with actual friends or with some peers you'd like to feel closer to. Picture the sights, sounds, and interactions happening around you.

What kinds of conversations do you value with them?

_____

_____

What are some uplifting things that others say or do but that you might not notice because you focus too much on how you come across to them?

_____

_____

How much more can you enjoy being with them if you let go of the need for their approval?

_____

_____

How can seeing the joy of others help you feel fulfilled and upbeat within yourself?

_____

_____

BOOSTING CONFIDENCE
FROM SOMEONE INSPIRING

It is easy to feel empty and hesitant when you also feel down and disconnected from others. Being happy with who you are is important when you reach out to others. Take a few breaths and think of one or two people you admire who have the confidence to be themselves. Now, just like a car battery being boosted by another with jumper cables, imagine borrowing some of that confidence from these people who inspire you. Combine that infusion of incoming confident energy with your own uniqueness. Hold this image of yourself while answering the following questions:

What unique inner qualities do you value about yourself and believe are valuable to others?

_____

_____

_____

How can having courage to stick out from the crowd help you feel surer of yourself?

_____

_____

_____

Think of that same person or someone else you admire for dressing or acting in ways that show they feel comfortable in their own skin. What role can being self-accepting play in connecting with others in deeper, more meaningful ways?

_____

_____

_____

How can realizing that social self-confidence is okay to keep working on, and something that you look for in a healthy way from both others and within yourself, change your perspective?

_____

_____

_____

COPING WITH A BREAK UP

The end of an intimate relationship can feel sad, empty, and overwhelming. Even if you are not currently in a breakup situation, it can help to examine the feelings you may have if you were in that situation. When coping with a breakup, mindfulness can soothe your overwhelmed, sadness-laden thoughts. It can really help just to accept whatever feelings come your way without judging them.

Just sit with whatever feelings come to mind as you imagine them splattering on the wall in front of you. You will notice some of the boxes contain feeling words, and some are empty. Think of words for feelings of your own to fill them in.

Sad	Hurt	Crushed

How did noticing, without judgment, your thoughts and feelings about this breakup help or not help you accept it?

_____

_____

In what ways can noticing your breakup-related struggles without judgment help you better understand why the relationship ended?

_____

_____

How does letting go of negative feelings help you heal from the pain of a breakup that initially leaves you feeling sad?

_____

_____

What can you learn about yourself by going through a difficult experience such as a breakup?

_____

_____

_____

NOTICING AND DISPUTING
YOUR SAD SOCIAL THOUGHTS

With cognitive behavioral therapy you can identify and challenge your sadness that comes from struggling in the social realm. This activity helps you to reframe how you react and feel in these situations.

Think of a social situation you felt sad about that occurred in the past few months. Put a check mark next to any of the following sadness-related feelings that were likely going on for you at the time:

___ Disappointed	___ Discouraged	___ Disempowered
___ Hopeless	___ Scared	___ Overwhelmed
___ Filled with Doubt	___ Hesitant	___ Defeated
___ Hurt	___ Let Down	___ Upset

What did you think in this situation, and how did thinking this way lead you to the above feelings?

_____

_____

_____

As time went on, what did you say to yourself about the situation that made it feel even worse for you?

_____

_____

_____

What is a better way to look at this situation to help you feel better?

_____

_____

_____

CHALLENGING SOCIALLY
NEGATIVE THOUGHTS

Sad, depressing thoughts can make it really hard to connect with others. Challenge each of the following counterproductive, hopelessness-generating thoughts with more positive ones. The first hopeless thought and its alternative healthier thought is provided for you as an example to use throughout the exercise.

Hopeless Thought

"I'm going to be stuck forever with no friends." (catastrophic conclusion)

Alternative Thought

"I have good relationships with my family members, and there is no reason I can't apply these skills to developing friendships."

· · · · · · · · · · · · · · · · · · ·

Hopeless Thought

"People look down on me because I have nothing to offer." (unfavorable comparison)

Alternative Thought

_____.

Hopeless Thought

"They always seem to know what to say and they're funny, and that leaves me feeling inferior." (all-or-nothing thinking and negative labeling)

Alternative Thought

_____.

Hopeless Thought

"That one person at the party ignored me and it ruined my whole time there." (negative filtering)

Alternative Thought

_____.

Hopeless Thought

"He did not respond my text right away, so he is probably not into me." (jumping to conclusions)

Alternative Thought

_____.

CHANGING A
SOCIAL SADNESS STORY

Cindy wants to better understand how her unhelpful thoughts about a social situation could get in her way. You can help her out by filling in more helpful ways for her to think and feel about the situation so that she does not feel rejected and sad.

While Cindy was walking through a school hallway, her new friend Yvonne passed her by and seemingly ignored her. She could have thought to herself, "Oh no! I can never keep any friends."

A healthier thought could have been: _____

_____.

Cindy's further accelerating negative thoughts may have led her to feelings of sadness, emptiness, and rejection. As an emotionally unhealthy way to cope with feeling rejected, Cindy could have chosen to ignore Yvonne.

A healthier behavior may have been: _____
when seeing her later on, because deep down she was scared of being further hurt and rejected by her. If she simply ignored Yvonne, though, Cindy would have likely felt

_____,
which only would have made her situation seem worse.

Now that you've filled in the blanks above, here's how Cindy herself used her CBT skills to handle the situation. When Yvonne actually passed her by, Cindy said to herself, "Wow, that was strange—but wait a minute, that's not like Yvonne. I'll try to catch her tomorrow and make sure she's doing okay." Cindy then reached out to Yvonne the next day to see if she was going through a rough time and could use some help. She did this by texting Yvonne after school to try and talk before homeroom the next morning.

When Cindy next saw her, Yvonne burst into tears and shared that a hot guy she liked was now dating another girl. In other words, when Yvonne had seemingly ignored Cindy, she was super preoccupied with feeling rejected and never even noticed her. Cindy felt a sense of fulfillment in this situation by identifying, disputing, and preventing socially destructive thoughts that could have created a rift with Yvonne when Yvonne was dealing with her own difficult situation.

Can you see how two very different ways of thinking about the same situation (thinking and feeling negatively vs. coping effectively) can generate different feelings and possibly different outcomes?

DEALING WITH
POPULARITY PERCEPTIONS

If you get saddened by not seeing yourself as one of the "popular kids," you are not alone. Not being on the homecoming court or not being a star athlete or an honor-roll student may leave you unfairly and distortedly thinking and feeling like you are "less than." As you'll see, though, a big part of managing social stress comes from feeling value within yourself, not from gauging how popular you think you are. When it comes to feeling socially fulfilled, sometimes it helps to realize that focusing on the quality of your existing social connections can be more fulfilling than focusing on a desire to be even more popular.

Ask yourself how often you hear the terms *popular* or *popularity*, and reflect on what they mean to you. As you do so, consider the following reflective questions to help you identify how, in your thoughts and behaviors, you may be negatively influenced by the term *popular*.

What does popularity represent to you?

_____

_____

What are some unhealthy ways that people strive to be popular?

_____

_____

How can the pressure to be popular lead you to self-pressuring and distorted thoughts that get in the way of knowing your own value?

_____

_____

How can focusing on the depth and quality of your friendships, rather than the quantity of them, leave you feeling more fulfilled?

_____

_____

COPING WITH SADNESS:

IT'S NO JOKE

Have you ever heard "Just kidding" or something similar after someone said something unpleasant to you disguised as a supposed joke? While someone may not intend to be hurtful, feeling put down can feel disheartening and saddening. It can not only be upsetting to be on the receiving end of a not-so-funny joke, but it can also be upsetting when you realize that a joke you've made has ended up hurting someone else.

Imagine that you are sitting down for lunch in the cafeteria and one of your presumed friends embarrasses you with a put-down comment. Now what?

Fill in more-helpful thoughts to challenge your upsetting thoughts, as shown in the first two examples:

"Everyone will think I'm pathetic!" vs. "I'm not the one who is putting someone down."

"I feel humiliated." vs. "I'm the one in charge of my pride, not them."

"I'm just socially awkward." vs. "_____

_____."

"I can't come up with a good comeback." vs. "_____

_____."

"There must be something really wrong with me that I get picked on all the time." vs.

"_____

_____."

"I hate having to be around people." vs. "_____

_____."

WOULD YOU CHOOSE
YOURSELF AS A FRIEND?

Refer to the list of your strengths on page 68 and reflect on which of these are treasured qualities that make you a good friend.

Do other people know about these qualities?

_____

_____

_____

What is something unique and interesting about you that you have hardly shared with others?

_____

_____

_____

How does knowing your strengths and interests help you connect with others?

_____

_____

_____

How do you limit your ability to feel fulfilled with friends or potential friends by losing sight of your strengths?

_____

_____

_____

FEELING THE BENEFITS OF
OPTIMISM FROM OTHERS

Optimism helps you escape social sadness by focusing on the potential and upside of your connections with others. Reflect on these questions to see how this can work for you.

How do you feel around people who hold a positive outlook?

_____

_____

_____

How does the positive, optimistic energy of other people affect you?

_____

_____

_____

What can you do to inspire positive energy in others? (For example, reflect on what goes well in their lives, compliment them, etc.)

_____

_____

_____

What would happen if you acted optimistic even if inwardly you were struggling with your confidence about connecting with others?

_____

_____

_____

LIFT YOUR MOOD
WITH GRATITUDE

Gratitude for your connections with peers and friends can go a long way in helping you feel more connected and less alone.

How does showing gratitude to friends encourage them to feel more connected to you?

_____

_____

_____

When was the last time you thanked a friend for something they did, or thanked them for their friendship?

_____

_____

_____

How do you think it felt for your friend to hear your gratitude?

_____

_____

_____

How did you feel expressing it?

_____

_____

_____

How does gratitude help you avoid "keeping score" in relationships?

_____

_____

_____

GRATITUDE FOR
DEEPER FRIENDSHIPS

It is common to take our friendships for granted at times. Valuing our friendships, though, makes them stronger and helps us feel less alone when we reflect on what we truly value in our friends.

Pick one friend and deeply reflect on the qualities you value in them and how it feels to notice them. Think of three positive experiences that occurred with this one special friend that would not have happened if you were not friends.

How does reflecting on good times with them and other close friends help to fill you up emotionally in a positive way?

_____

_____

_____

What would be the downside of not expressing your appreciation to this friend?

_____

_____

_____

How can expressing appreciation to your close friends lower feelings of sadness you may be experiencing?

_____

_____

_____

CONNECT WITH OTHERS
USING OPTIMISM

Reflect on how it feels for you when you listen to others who tend to communicate in pessimistic ways. For example:

- "I can't really trust anyone because I get disappointed when I do."
- "I'll never make any friends in college."
- "No one really cares about me."
- "Things always go wrong in my life."

Can you see how frequently hearing pessimistic vibes from someone can be a downer?

_____

_____

Now reflect on someone you know who tends to be optimistic. Most likely they:

- don't overly blame themselves when things go wrong.
- realize that setbacks are temporary.
- give themselves appropriate credit when they do things well.

Do you tend to present yourself to others in a more pessimistic or optimistic manner?

_____

_____

Think of a time when someone may have benefited from you being more optimistic when they came to you for support. How did they feel in response to your encouragement?

_____

_____

How does being optimistic make you a better friend?

_____

_____

MINDFULNESS FOR BODY-IMAGE SADNESS

A study by Jennifer Todd, a British researcher, suggests that the more we tune in to what is going on inside our bodies, the better we may feel about them on the outside. This, in turn, suggests that if we learn to notice our bodies from the inside, we can be less critical about them, feel less sadness tied to how we look, and have an improved body image. The body scan is a wonderful mindfulness activity to help you learn how to tune in to your body in this valuable new way.

BODY SCAN TO
LET GO OF SADNESS

Familiarize yourself with the body scan by reading the instructions below. Then record yourself reading the instructions and play it back. Another option is to have a partner (such as a friend or family member) read the instructions aloud while you do the body scan, and then switch roles to take turns.

Before you begin the body scan, you may want to make sure that you're wearing comfortable, loose-fitting clothing so that you can feel relaxed and tune in better to your internal sensations rather than the feeling of your clothes. I also recommend that you remove your shoes. As you scan your body, you may notice sensations such as discomfort, tension, aches, pains, coldness, or stiffness. And you may also notice the opposite: soothing sensations, muscle relaxation, warmth, or looseness.

You may also observe that some parts of your body feel energized, while other parts feel tired. Or you may notice no sensations at all. What's cool about the body scan is that you don't have to feel pressure to say it works. There's no goal other than noticing the sensations in your body in a new way. But by tuning in to your body without judgment, you'll likely feel calmer because you're not focused on your worries.

Let's begin. Go to a place where you can comfortably lie down on your back—for example, lie on your bed, a soft rug or carpet, or a mat. Keep your arms by your sides, palms facing up, legs gently apart, and close your eyes if that feels comfortable. Some teens tell me they feel more comfortable placing a pillow under their knees or just raising their knees in a bent position. Feel free to experiment with your position—you may even prefer to sit up.

1. Gently bring awareness to your body. Notice your body on the surface you're lying on, without judging whether your body feels lighter or heavier than normal. Notice the places your body is touching. Also notice as you breathe out, perhaps, a sense of yourself gently sinking a little deeper into the mat, bed, or chair.

2. Notice how your breath feels, including its movement within your body as you breathe in and out. Feel the warmth of your breath, if you can, going in and out of your nose. You may also notice your chest or belly rising or falling. Continue being gently aware of your breath for a few minutes. Just know that it is normal for your mind to wander during the body scan. When it does, gently refocus on your breath.

3. When you're ready, shift your focus to your left leg, moving all the way down your leg to below your big toe. Notice the sensations in your toes with a new sense of curiosity. Move your attention to your big toe, your little toe, and then the rest of your toes. What do they feel like? Do they tingle, not seem noticeable, or feel different in some other way? Are they tight or loose, or warm or cold? As you breathe in, imagine gently sending your breath down your body and into your toes.

As you breathe out, imagine your breath going back up your body and out through your nose. Apply this way of moving your breath to each part of your body. Now move your awareness to the bottom of your foot. Notice the ball and heel. Does either feel heavy or light? As you move your attention to the sides and upper part of your left foot and ankle, pay attention to the sensations you feel in these areas. Draw your breath into all parts of your left foot. As you become aware of these sensations, gently let them go when you feel ready.

4. Move to the lower part of your left leg, knee, and upper leg, continuing to bring in the same intention of gentle, curious, accepting awareness.

5. In noticing your left leg in this special way, feel how the sensations in it may seem different from those in your right leg.

6. Gently shift your awareness up and down your right leg, extending down to your toes with a similar path of traveling awareness, and then move back up to your upper leg in the same way that you did with your left. Then let it go.

7. Now tune in to your pelvis area, hips, and buttocks. Notice what this area of your body feels like.

8. Move up to your lower torso, lower abdomen, and lower back. Notice how your belly feels as you breathe in and out. Welcome any emotions you feel here. Greet these gut feelings by exploring and accepting them as they are.

9. Gently shift your attention to your chest and upper back. With a sense of curiosity, notice and feel your rib cage rising and falling as you breathe in and out. Tune in to the beating of your heart. If you can, notice any emotions you are experiencing. Feel grateful for all the surrounding vital organs that are keeping you alive. Allow any of your emotions that arise to express themselves.

10. Move your focus to both of your arms, beginning with your fingertips and moving up to your shoulders. Continue to breathe into and out of each body part before you move to the next one.

11. Gently move your awareness to your neck. After noticing your neck in this special way, move your awareness to your facial muscles, including your jaw, which often holds a lot of worry-related tension. Just notice whether this area feels tight or loose.

12. Move your awareness to the rest of your head, nonjudgmentally noticing it in this special way.

13. Gently send your breath up and down your body from your head to your feet, and vice versa. Notice your breath as it freely travels within you, moving up and down your body. Feel the centering energy by letting your breath flow within you in this way.

14. Just let yourself be as you are. Simply rest and relax for a few minutes in this gentle, peaceful place that you have discovered within yourself.

Did you want to continue noticing your body in this special way, or did you start to feel bored?

_____

_____

Did you feel more positively connected to your body when you took time to notice it in a special way?

_____

_____

Are you feeling lighter, happier, less stressed out, or filled with energy?

_____

_____

Are you pleased with the way you felt during and after the body scan, or are you disappointed with the experience?

_____

_____

Regardless of the outcome, how can you feel proud and grateful for giving yourself the opportunity to notice your body in this special way?

_____

_____

Starting with your toes and moving up to your head is the most popular way of doing the body scan, but in the future, you may reverse the order if you prefer to. One colleague of mine starts with her head, claiming it helps relax her mind better, and then she works down to her toes.

The body scan, and the special awareness you get from it, is always available for you to revisit and reexperience. Each time you do it will likely feel a little different, depending on what's going on with you that day.

By noticing your body without judgment, you'll learn to manage all sorts of bodily discomfort and to lessen any physical pain that you're feeling as a result of your worries. Teens tell me that the body scan also helps them see the connections between their emotions and physical sensations, which is key to overall health. I hope you give this wonderful exercise a fair chance. Remember that one of the beautiful things about mindfulness is that you don't have to judge the process or the results. Just patiently observe them as best as you can.

MAKING FRIENDS
WITH YOUR BODY

Take a few gentle breaths and imagine the concern and caring energy you feel for friends whom you value. As you do this, reflect on the following questions:

How does caring about someone you value positively influence the way that you see them?

_____

_____

_____

In contrast, when you don't think of someone in a caring way, can you see how you might be out of touch with the positive qualities that person brings to the world?

_____

_____

_____

Now reflect on how considering your body as your friend feels to you. Does seeing your body as your close friend raise its value to you?

_____

_____

_____

Can you see how not being mindful of the value of your friendship with someone and neglecting the way you value your body are similar?

_____

_____

_____

GETTING MINDFUL ABOUT YOUR BODY IN THE RAIN

Let's bring in some more RAIN for this next activity. Here is a refresher for what this acronym means:

R: Recognize

A: Allow

I: Inquire and investigate

N: Not totally defining yourself (The exercise will explain.)

As presented earlier, RAIN promotes recognizing, allowing, investigating, and not overidentifying with the sensations you feel in your body as a result of sadness (or as a result of anything else, for that matter). When it comes to being mindful of what is going on in your body, you will find it helpful to be in the RAIN.

WASHING AWAY
BODY-IMAGE SADNESS

Approach this RAIN activity with a beginner's mind of being curious and accepting of whatever the RAIN feels like to you. Keep a flexible mindset for how long you stay in the RAIN. I suggest that you spend a few minutes in each of the four steps. If, however, you move through some steps more slowly or quickly than others, that is okay, too. Just welcome a sense of nonjudgmental mindfulness to connect with your body. While keeping these thoughts and feelings in mind, let's get into the RAIN.

Recognize: Take a few deep breaths, and then focus your attention on your body. How is your body feeling right now? Try to recognize what's going on related to the body parts you are sad about. Notice beneath the surface as well as at the surface itself (your skin). Is your body sending you signals of any sort? Are there any areas where you notice a feeling of tension? Any areas where you notice feeling relaxed? Do any parts of your body feel warm or cold? Are you experiencing any pressure sensations or pain?

Allow: Allow the sensations in your body to be there. If you feel an urge to yawn or scratch an itch, just notice it and most likely it will go away. Don't judge any bodily sensations as good or bad. Don't dwell on what they might mean. Just accept that they're present right now, without trying to fight or suppress them.

Inquire and Investigate: Ask yourself whether the sensations in your body are familiar or perhaps new to you. Try to feel a deep awareness of each sensation, observing how it changes or moves over time.

Not Totally Defining Yourself: Notice the sensations in your body as just one part of your overall being. These sensations have not *always* been with you. You won't continue to experience these exact same sensations *forever*. The fact is, they're simply passing through. They're not an enduring part of who you are. You're not stuck with them. You are more than the feelings in your body. Think about that for a while.

What sensations, if any, did you notice in your body?

_____

_____

_____

How did it feel to notice your bodily sensations without judgment?

_____

_____

_____

Did RAIN help lessen your focus on your sad feelings related to your body image?

_____

_____

_____

How could doing this activity in the future be helpful to you when you are struggling with sadness related to body image?

_____

_____

_____

Now that you're in the RAIN, if you want to further explore the impact of negatively comparing your body image to others and the resulting sadness, you can do the following:

R: Recognize any desires to compare yourself physically to your peers. This can include, for example, thoughts of feeling inadequate and defective.

A: Allow yourself to notice these thoughts without trying to fight or suppress them, just accept them.

I: Inquire and investigate how these thoughts of negative comparison and inadequacy make you feel. In the context of this discussion, this could mean feeling inadequate and sad.

N: Not totally define yourself by asking: "Does comparing how I look to my peers have value to me? Do I have to let these thoughts and feelings define how I see myself, or can I embrace more positive thoughts and feelings about my appearance?"

CBT FOR BODY-IMAGE SADNESS

Cognitive behavioral therapy can help you further deal with feelings of sadness you may have related to body-image struggles. For example, do you feel alone when wondering why some of your less-attractive peers don't seem especially concerned about the way they look? And why is it, on the other hand, that some really attractive people feel disheartened about the tiniest details? It's because, when it comes to your body image, how you think about and view your appearance plays a huge role. Flawed thinking, not a flawed body, is at the core of your self-esteem issues related to body image.

Check out the following sadness-oriented unhealthy and alternative healthy thoughts about body image in the table below.

Sad, Discouraging Body-Image Thought	Healthy, Reasonable Thought
I must have a perfect body or else peers won't notice me or like me.	*Wait, I like kids who don't have perfect bodies, and it helps to realize that obviously other people do, too. And if someone doesn't like me because I don't look a certain way, then they really aren't worth my time because their priorities are screwed up.*
My body is really awful because of [insert "flaw" here].	*Okay, hold on. Yes, maybe I don't have a thigh gap and my stomach might not be flat, but that doesn't mean that I'm unattractive.*
I'm worthless because all that seems to really count is how you look, and my body is not perfect like those girls that everyone thinks are hot.	*Just because these societal ideals exist does not mean I can't also exist in a good way, too. My character and how I treat others count a ton for how I look to others, even if my body isn't ideal.*
I so hate my body because I wish it was like the beautiful bodies I see in the hallways and on social media.	*It's unfair to hate my body just because it's not perfect. Very few people have the seemingly "perfect genes" to look like that!*
I'm not masculine enough. I don't look like those guys with wide shoulders and big arms.	*Muscles aren't the only thing that make a man—men are more than just their bodies.*

SEEING YOURSELF IN
A BRIGHTER LIGHT

Identifying and challenging your unfair and harsh thoughts about your appearance is the first step in using CBT to alleviate body-image sadness. Follow the examples from the table on the previous page as you reflect on the following questions:

What is a sad thought you have that results from being critical of your body?

_____

_____

_____

Now describe a more reasonable and supportive way to reframe this thought.

_____

_____

_____

How does it feel to write down and counter this unhealthy, sadness-provoking thought about how you look?

_____

_____

_____

How can changing the way you think and feel about your body image raise your overall self-esteem?

_____

_____

_____

COUNTERING BODY-IMAGE MYTHS

Body-image dissatisfaction has been relatively common for some time, but sadness related to how our bodies look has more recently been linked to how we negatively compare our bodies to the societal ideals we see in the media.

What follows are appearance-related myths you may identify with that are distorted, sadness-triggering beliefs about body image. Counter each of these thoughts following the example of the first one listed.

Distorted Thought:

"If you are really good-looking, your life is happier."

More Reasonable Thought:

"Life is much more than how I look or how I measure up to the looks of others."

Distorted Thought:

"People see my physical flaws first, and that puts me at a disadvantage."

More Reasonable Thought:

_____

Distorted Thought:

"These great-looking people never have anything to feel sad about. They always look so happy."

More Reasonable Thought:

_____

Distorted Thought:

"By changing how I look, I could find true happiness."

More Reasonable Thought:

_____

Distorted Thought:

"My looks are what hold me back from good things coming my way."

More Reasonable Thought:

_____

POSITIVE PSYCHOLOGY FOR BODY-IMAGE SADNESS

Here's a fail-safe, instant body-image picker-upper—maintaining good posture.

Slouching is a common teenage "affliction" that can leave you feeling tired, defeated, and down. You may slouch because of your feelings about your body image, but being mindful to straighten up with good, strong posture can actually pick up your mood. That's because good posture helps you feel more confident. And others will see you as more confident in response to your more self-assured posture.

And, more important, good posture is also *physically* healthy — it promotes healthy circulation, increased lung capacity, and healthy joints, and it helps to ease bodily tension and pain. Good posture also promotes improved mental health. It is really cool that physically adjusting and correcting your posture actually addresses some of the very body-image issues that teens torture themselves with, which are often worsened by having poor posture.

POSITIONING YOURSELF FOR
BETTER POSTURE

Improving your posture can make you feel better and look better!

1. Breathe in and out mindfully a few times.

2. Sit up or stand up, and look at yourself in a full-length or large mirror, noticing your posture. Are you leaning to the side? Are you slumped? Are you sitting/standing straight?

3. Breathe in confidence by imagining holding yourself straight and tall like a strong tree, and shift to sit or stand as straight as you can.

4. Hold this improved posture and reflect on how you feel. How does your body feel different when you hold a confident posture? How do you feel emotionally?

How did shifting to a better posture feel to you?

_____

_____

_____

Can you see how the posture of others impacts how you experience their moods as well?

_____

_____

_____

Would carrying yourself with better posture be a quick way to feel better when you are feeling sad?

_____

_____

_____

FEELING GRATITUDE FOR YOUR BODY

One way to boost your mood if you are feeling sad about your body is to feel gratitude for how it functions and what it does for you. The more you cherish how your body works for you, the more you will value all aspects of it, including its appearance.

What is something amazing your body has allowed you to do in the last few months? For example, did you run a race, go on a hike, take a long walk with a friend, or accomplish something cool while playing a sport or making music?

_____

_____

_____

How does it feel to be grateful for your body—an awesome, spectacularly designed human machine that is at your service 24 hours a day, seven days a week?

_____

_____

_____

How can feeling good about your body's physical health help your emotional health?

_____

_____

_____

MINDFULNESS FOR FAMILY-RELATED SADNESS

Home is a place in which we seek to share a sense of comfort and peace with our family. But while your family is hopefully an important source of love, joy, and support for you, it probably doesn't always feel this way.

Although you likely love your parents and siblings, you can probably agree that sometimes family members can drive you crazy and leave you feeling down. Annoying quirks and mannerisms, unwelcome comments or unsolicited advice, conflicts over possessions or personal space, and joking that goes too far are examples of those not-so-warm-and-cozy, disheartening moments of family life. Let's look to mindfulness for some ways to feel happier when family issues are pulling you down.

FLOATING AWAY FROM
FAMILY TENSIONS

Recall having a disagreement or conflict of some kind with a family member that made you feel sad. As you reflect on this experience, notice your thoughts, feelings, and behaviors at the time. Now imagine you and your family member being lifted up and then floating above the spot where you were experiencing this conflict.

As you floated above the conflict, did it feel like the burden of this experience became lighter for you?

_____

_____

_____

What are some ways that being less reactive with your emotions might actually result in less intense and fewer conflicts with this family member? Would you become happier?

_____

_____

_____

How can rising up in your mind help you take the emotionally lighter road with family members you struggle with?

_____

_____

_____

What fun things could you now do with family members after letting go of sadness-related tensions?

_____

_____

_____

LETTING THE SUN SHINE ON
YOUR FAMILY TREE

Put a different spin on the term *family tree*. Rather than tracing back the roots of your family, in this tool you will imagine strengthening it with warm sunshine.

> *Reflect on the image of a solid tree to represent your family.*
>
> *See the leaves gently swaying in the breeze.*
>
> *Imagine negative family energy flowing out through the leaves and into the surrounding air.*
>
> *Visualize warm, gentle rays of sun now nourishing the leaves.*
>
> *Focus on this image for a few minutes.*

How did you feel toward your family while doing this activity?

_____

_____

_____

How does visualizing the warm sunlight on the leaves brighten your mood when reflecting on your family?

_____

_____

_____

What is the upside of mindfully focusing on positive images, such as you did here, when you are going through rough times with your family?

_____

_____

_____

How can pausing and focusing on a nurturing image help you gain control of your sad and overwhelming emotions when you're amid difficult family situations?

_____

_____

_____

EVALUATING YOUR
FAMILY FRUSTRATIONS

CBT can help you get in touch with difficult thoughts and feelings that arise when you feel sad and empty about things going on in your family.

Consider the following questions to examine the impact of your thoughts about your family as they influence any sad feelings you experience. Reflect on what you are saying to yourself about them.

Are you being fair or thinking in a counterproductive way?

_____

_____

_____

What do you expect from your parents and siblings that is reasonable, and what expectations might not be reasonable?

_____

_____

_____

Do you make negative comparisons between your family and other families you see in a more idealized way? If so, how does that play a role in the sad feelings you may have about your own family?

_____

_____

_____

How does it help reduce your sadness when you remind yourself that every family is made up of individuals who have limitations?

_____

_____

_____

REDUCING SADNESS
FROM PARENT CONFLICT WITH CBT

When you're feeling upset and frustrated about your parents' rules and restrictions, call on CBT to calm you down. Imagine any situation where you feel that your parents are hindering you from doing something you want to do.

What are your sad, upsetting thoughts and feelings that come along with this situation? For example, maybe you feel like "They just won't let me do anything" (all-or-nothing thinking). Or "Mom is impossible" (negative labeling). Or "This is why I don't want to be nice, because they are never nice to me" (jumping to conclusions). Or "All I see is them pressuring me" (negative filtering). Can you see that burdening your mind with things like negative filtering and all-or-nothing thinking feeds your sad feelings?

What are some of the ways you shut down or act out when your sad thoughts and feelings get the best of you?

_____

_____

_____

Can you see how being tuned in to your upsetting thoughts and feelings and then challenging them will help you get along better with your parents?

_____

_____

_____

How does being more flexible in your thinking help you to see things more from their perspective?

_____

_____

_____

STRENGTHEN YOUR FAMILY

The strengths-based focus of positive psychology offers valuable tools to help you offset feelings of sadness and emptiness that you may feel about your family as a whole, or specific family members.

Take a few moments and reflect on the strengths you bring to your family. Now check out the following list of strengths and circle any that resonate with you:

Enthusiastic	Motivated	Organized
Reliable	Determined	Detail-Oriented
Trustworthy	Dedicated	Attentive
Creative	Honest	Patient
Disciplined	Easygoing	Open-Minded
Patient	Good Communicator	Humorous
Spiritual	Practical	Kind
Perceptive	Flexible	Caring

Consider the following questions to help you reflect on your strengths:

How does it feel to take a few minutes to get in touch with the strengths you bring to your family?

_____

_____

What accomplishments are you most proud of with family members, and which of your strengths helped you achieve them?

_____

_____

When did you lose sight of the strengths you have that may have helped others in your family cope with struggles or sadness?

_____

_____

How can knowing your strengths help you use them with your family in the future?

_____

_____

SEEING PAST SADNESS
AND SEE YOUR FAMILY'S STRENGTHS

Let's look at a way to alleviate sadness about what you feel you may not be getting from your family by giving them credit for the strengths they bring to your life. Consider the following questions:

What is a quality you admire about a family member whom you also find difficult at times?

_____

_____

_____

How can being appreciative of that person's positive offerings help you feel less sad, negative energy with them?

_____

_____

_____

What is the benefit to not waiting for someone in your family to "go first" in terms of trying to bridge misunderstandings and work through past disappointments?

_____

_____

_____

How can focusing on the strengths of your family as a whole help you feel more connected to everyone in it?

_____

_____

_____

How does focusing on what you contribute to your family's strengths help you to feel better about yourself?

_____

_____

_____

GOING WITH THE
FAMILY FLOW

Doing some exercise will increase your brain's feel-good neurotransmitters, called endorphins. And doing it with a family member can be a great way to feel refreshed and reconnected within your family as well.

Exercise is also really cool because moving and focusing on your body gets you tuned in to the present moment, which switches you from feeling sad about the past or the future. Walking or running casually or for time or distance, lifting weights, or doing any other kind of physical activity gives you a sense of immersion in what you are doing in the moment.

And connecting to a family member through being in the moment together can really help to get you out of feeling unfulfilled or sad about past times or the future. The bottom line is that the more you move, and get absorbed in doing so, the less sadness you'll probably feel.

What kind of exercise would feel good to you to do with a family member?

_____

_____

When would be a good time for you and family members to exercise?

_____

_____

How often would you be open to exercising?

_____

_____

What would be an obstacle to exercising?

_____

_____

How can you overcome that obstacle?

_____

_____

Part C | # MANAGING ANGER

GETTING TO KNOW ANGER

Anger bubbles up from your reactive brain as a result of a fight reaction to feeling threatened. The emotion of anger is very different from anxiety and depression, which we experience as more of a sense of feeling internally weighed down. In contrast, anger is usually a reaction of wanting to express yourself or act in response to a threat, which may be real or imagined. Depending on the circumstances that evoke it, anger, like other emotions, ranges in intensity.

The main topics of this workbook—school pressures, social situations, body-image concerns, and family issues—can trigger anger just as they can be sources of anxiety and depression. Anger itself is not a bad feeling—it is part of what makes us human. Our angry feelings resulting from daily pressures and stresses are a normal experience for all of us.

For example, maybe your parents occasionally want you to spend more time with family than you do with friends, and you may feel annoyed. In this case, while your parents may have a valid concern, your anger is likely about feeling that your time with friends is threatened. This is an example of what is commonly referred to as *situational anger*, which comes up when you feel vulnerable or overwhelmed and you react to protect yourself. As the perceived threat seems less overwhelming, your anger usually fades.

Anger is frequently misunderstood, however, because it is often seen as destructive. Although anger can feel intense or even overwhelming, that does not mean it is bad. In fact, anger has positive effects for us at times—when it is managed well. For example, anger has likely played a valuable role in leading to safety measures undertaken at schools as a result of horrific shooting events that imposed trauma on many innocent victims. And, from a historical perspective, appropriately channeled anger has paved the way in forming social equality movements for oppressed people throughout the world, including the American civil rights movement, women's rights advocacy groups, and many others.

The more you learn to understand anger, the more you can manage it. Just like managing feelings of anxiety and depression, this takes some awareness and practice. To manage your anger, you need to look and listen carefully to what is going on. Anger signals you to stick up for yourself and others in acceptable ways.

UNDERSTANDING YOUR ANGRY BRAIN

When you feel threatened and react with anger, your body jumps into the fight, flight, or freeze mode we discussed earlier. Have you ever felt as though your anger gave you an "out of body" experience? Your reactive brain may feel like it wants you to scream at someone, or flip a desk at school, or just stomp off. This surge of anger is due to the release of adrenaline, which gives you that burst of energy. When this happens, your pupils dilate, your heart accelerates, your blood pressure rises, and your breathing speeds up. You become super focused on what is going on around you. This comes from your reactive brain instinctively trying to protect you from a perceived threatening situation.

Depending on what you are reacting to, your anger can come upon you quickly, or it can build up over time. Either way, a key aspect of managing anger is realizing that it is an emotion that can be harmful or helpful, like many others. Attempting to will your anger away, or trying to ignore it, however, usually puts you on that sure-to-fail, "bottle it up and explode later" plan (and this is true for anxiety and depression as well).

Managing your anger takes self-awareness when you're experiencing it. Even learning to pause a few seconds before you react with anger is very helpful.

One of the problems with anger comes from trying to stop it without really knowing how to do so constructively. We often are not mindful of our emerging anger, and then it just comes "out of the blue." Trying to stop anger can feel like trying to catch a boulder-sized snowball as it gathers momentum rolling down a hill during an avalanche. It can end up feeling like it is coming your way and will swallow you up once it is out of control.

Speaking of "out of control"—as a young child you likely threw a tantrum when things did not go your way. But as a teen, you have developed more insight to be aware and reflect on what is going on inside you and around you when you feel anger. Part of your learned insight is from you being aware of the other words commonly used to describe anger.

We've already discussed how anxiety and depression have a personal meaning to you, and so does anger. While you have awareness of these anger-signaling words, the more familiar you are with what you think and express when you're feeling angry, the more you will be ready to use anger-management tools. In short, just being aware of the words going on in your mind when you are angry is a great start in learning to control your anger.

RECOGNIZING
ANGER'S ALIASES

Reflect on times you feel angry and the things you say when you are feeling it. To help you do this, take a look at the list of words and phrases that are often used to describe anger. Notice the blank spaces for adding your own additional words.

I'm really pissed off
Stop it
I'm gonna give them crap
I can't believe they did that
I'm so-o-o fed up
You can't make this sh!t up
This is so frustrating
I'm sick of it
Not having it
This sucks
It's so unfair
I feel betrayed

I'm jealous
I'm aggravated
I hate this
I'm mad
I'm disgusted
I'm going nuts
No way
C'mon, seriously
They are awful
I can't stand it
That's bullsh!t
What the ___fuck___

_____   _____

Which words or phrases represent what you are thinking when you express anger?

_____

_____

With whom and in what places and times do you outwardly express some of these words or other terms when you are feeling angry? Which ones do you say?

_____

_____

With whom and in which times and places do you try not to say some of these words?

_____

_____

What did you learn about yourself when reflecting on the words you use internally and verbalize outwardly to express your anger?

_____

_____

No matter what words you use to describe anger, it needs to be managed with healthy expectations. Otherwise, it ends up making your life or others' lives difficult or even regrettably worse. Let's take a quick, realistic look at how your expectations about anger do or don't help you manage it.

Anger Is Effectively Managed by . . .	Anger Is Poorly Managed by . . .
Expressing it.	Holding it in.
Using effective coping strategies to manage it, including mindfulness, CBT, and positive psychology.	Waiting for it to "just go away."
Seeing it as an opportunity to be aware of strong thoughts and feelings.	Continuing to dwell on it, repeatedly sharing negative feelings with others in an unconstructive way, or lashing out at others.
Realizing the situations where you tend to have various intensities of anger.	Globally labeling yourself as an "angry person."
Openly learning from occasions when anger has hurt you or others you know.	Rigidly rationalizing and justifying why you have been entitled to feel angry.
Reflecting on what has helped you to calm down in the past.	Refusing to give yourself credit for the times you have more effectively managed your anger in the past and seeing that you can build upon those positive situations.

TRACING YOUR
ANGER TRIGGERS

Now let's consider the types of situations in which you get angry. One way to do this is to notice your anger triggers—anything that influences you to feel angry and think angry thoughts. As you learn what things "push your buttons," you will be more able to understand the threatening situations that you react to with anger.

Consider each of the common anger-triggering situations below, circle the ones that you can relate to, and then write how often this occurs (daily, a few times per week, once a week, every two weeks, once a month or less), and how intense the anger can be for you, from 1 = low intensity to 10 = high intensity. Next, answer the questions that follow.

School: assignments, tests, presentations, teacher expectations, extracurricular demands

Trigger Situation _____   Trigger Situation _____

How Often?   _____   How Often?   _____

Intensity level?   _____   Intensity level?   _____

Social: being rejected, interrupted, threatened, compared, dismissed, cheated, pressured

Trigger Situation _____   Trigger Situation _____

How Often?   _____   How Often?   _____

Intensity level?   _____   Intensity level?   _____

Body-image concerns: underweight, overweight, skin, tall, short, hairstyle, other

Trigger Situation _____   Trigger Situation _____

How Often?   _____   How Often?   _____

Intensity level?   _____   Intensity level?   _____

Family conflicts: siblings, parents, other relatives, being nagged, privacy violated

Trigger Situation _____   Trigger Situation _____

How Often?   _____   How Often?   _____

Intensity level?   _____   Intensity level?   _____

Other (work, activities, politics, world events)

Trigger Situation _____ Trigger Situation _____

How Often? _____ How Often? _____

Intensity level? _____ Intensity level? _____

Having now identified some of your anger triggers, how can seeing the impact of the different situations you get angry about help you to manage them better?

_____

_____

_____

Why is it easy to fall back into being triggered over these types of situations even when we become aware that we may react in an angry manner?

_____

_____

_____

What can you do to maintain awareness of potential anger-triggering situations?

_____

_____

_____

Anger is referred to as a secondary emotion because it is linked to feelings that underlie it. When you feel triggered to become angry, this is usually linked to other underlying emotions first coming into play, emotions that we find hard to express directly.

WHAT'S UNDER YOUR ANGER?

Some common feelings that live below the surface of anger and that get sparked by your anger triggers are included in the list below. As you look over this list, note any of these feelings that you believe lead to occasions when you get angry.

Write them on the sides of the anger volcano below. You can see that some physiological states (which trigger anger as well), such as being hungry or tired, are also included, and so are some blank lines where you can add other underlying emotions or physiological states.

Frustration   Rejection   Attacked

Fear   Distrust   Pressured

Hurt   Jealousy   Trapped

Failure   Inadequacy   Tired

Humiliation   Insecurity   Provoked

Shame   Hungry   Disrespected

Sadness   Lonely   Vulnerable

Which of these feelings most often underlie your anger when you are experiencing it?

_____

_____

_____

What gets in the way of being aware of the feelings that lie beneath anger?

_____

_____

_____

How can knowing the feelings that underlie your anger help you to manage it?

_____

_____

_____

HOW DO YOU ACT
WHEN YOU'RE ANGRY?

Now that you have identified the ways you express anger in those triggering situations that come your way, let's explore the behaviors you engage in when you feel angry.

Check out the unhealthy ways people react when they feel angry, and put a circle around any you have done or still do at times. Fill in any other behaviors that may also apply to you on the blank lines below.

Become Argumentative	Tease or Mock Others
Obsess	Get Passive-Aggressive
Throw Things	Act Stubborn
Stare at Someone	Make Impulsive Decisions
Use Profanity	Become Demanding
Cry	Use Drugs
Raise Your Voice / Scream	Blame Others Unfairly
Punch, Kick, or Stomp	Withdraw
Become Defensive	Say That You're Tired
Become Sarcastic	Stare Off at Nothing
Ignore	Make Unrealistic Promises

_____   _____

With whom, where, and when do you tend to act out your anger in these ways?

_____

_____

_____

How do your behaviors affect the situation and people you are feeling angry about?

_____

_____

_____

What differences do you see in how you angrily react, depending on whom you are reacting to?

_____

_____

_____

What do you think and feel when other people behave in one or more of these negative ways?

_____

_____

_____

Reflect on a time when you initially may have wanted to act out negatively in response to experiencing anger and you are glad you didn't do so.

_____

_____

_____

Aggressive, Passive-Aggressive, and Assertive

Sometimes it is hard to understand whether our angry reactions are aggressive, passive-aggressive, or assertive. *Aggressive* behaviors are those where we trample over the rights of others. *Passive-aggressive* actions occur when we act more covertly to discharge our anger. *Assertive* behaviors are those where we stand up for our own rights without violating the rights of others. Look at the table below to see the differences among aggressive, passive-aggressive, and assertive behaviors.

BEHAVIOR

Aggressive	Passive-Aggressive	Assertive
Speaking forcefully	Silently resenting	Being direct
Criticizing	Cutting	Stating needs clearly
Interrupting	Backstabbing	Being respectful but confident
Unfairly blaming	Undermining	Asking to clarify
Shaming	Being sarcastic	Using appropriate tone
Overpowering	Playing the victim	Valuing problem-solving

EXPLORING BEHAVIORAL RESPONSES

Describe times when you were aggressive, passive-aggressive, or assertive (using the chart on the previous page as a guide).

_____

_____

_____

How did being aggressive work for you in that situation?

_____

_____

_____

What did your passive-aggressive response produce when you reacted that way?

_____

_____

_____

How did being assertive impact a situation you used it in?

_____

_____

_____

Which way of reacting helps others understand your position better and why?

_____

_____

_____

How do each of these different ways of responding when you are angry influence others to want either to pull away or get closer to you?

_____

_____

_____

How does being aggressive, passive-aggressive, or assertive lower or raise your self-esteem?

_____

_____

_____

In what ways does your negative reaction to anger lead to other feelings, such as embarrassment, guilt, shame, or remorse?

_____

_____

_____

How does the way you assertively react to anger lead to other positive feelings such as relief, confidence, satisfaction, pride, or gratitude?

_____

_____

_____

In what other ways does mismanaged anger vs. well-managed anger affect your friendships, significant others, family members, and the people you associate with in after-school activities and jobs?

_____

_____

_____

ANGER IN YOUR BODY

Like anxiety and depression, anger is an emotion that is expressed in your body in a number of physical ways. Paying attention to these bodily signals of anger can help you know when you are triggered. Circle any of the physical anger symptoms that you experience at times:

Tightness in Your Chest	Shaky Hands	Tight Hands
Tightness in Your Throat	Trembling Voice	Tense Feet
Neck Pain	Pounding in Chest	Upset Stomach
Sweaty Palms	Nausea	Dizziness
Backache	Dry Mouth	Stomachache
General Muscle Tension	Sleep Problems	Rapid Heart Rate
Butterflies in Your Stomach	Headache	Sweating
Faster Breathing	Warm Cheeks	Shaking
	Shoulder Tension	Spinning Sensation
	Jaw Tension	Pounding Feeling in Head

_____   _____   _____

Keeping in mind your responses to the list above, answer the following questions about how your body reacts to anger.

What parts of your body most often feel anger?

_____

_____

In the last two weeks, how frequently have you noticed anger in those parts of your body (e.g., many times a day, a few times a day, several days per week, a few days per week, weekly, or rarely)?

_____

How can being more aware of anger in those parts of your body help you to manage it?

_____

Going forward, which bodily signs of anger will be easiest to tune in to compared to others?

_____

UNMANAGED ANGER CAN HURT YOUR HEALTH

Anger can express itself through your body in many ways. When you become angry, your autonomic nervous system is aroused in response to you feeling threatened. The physiological reactions listed previously, when repeatedly occurring over time, can lead to health conditions such as high blood pressure, gastrointestinal distress, and chronic headaches. Anger can also worsen your feelings of anxiety and depression when you stew over unresolved issues and feel helpless or overwhelmed by them.

MEET YOUR ANGER METER

The more you can gauge just how angry you are feeling at any given time, the more you can avoid letting anger make you explode. This is crucial to managing your relationships with others, being able to strive toward goals in healthy ways when you're faced with challenges, and managing both your mental and physical health.

You've probably had a health-care provider take your blood pressure to see whether it is at a healthy level. Unfortunately, there is no current phone app or watch to put somewhere on your body to measure your anger as you would your blood pressure. But we can use our own anger thermometer as a gauge to monitor the range of our anger at any given time. Below are the levels of anger, represented here by Calm, Irritated, Upset, and Furious. Each is described below.

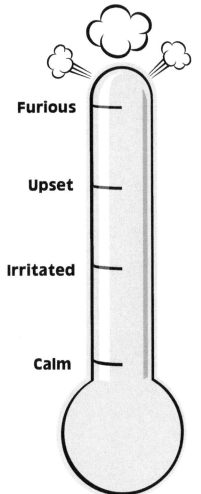

Calm (no anger at all)

This is when you feel relaxed and healthy. You get a little frustrated here and there but it fades quickly, and overall you feel good. When you're feeling calm, your likely behaviors might include hanging out with friends or enjoying your time by yourself listening to music and feeling good.

Irritated (mild to moderate anger)

When you are feeling irritated, you notice that you feel stirrings of anger. Your irritated behaviors likely might include avoiding others who you feel are trying your patience.

Upset (serious anger)

You are beyond moderate levels of anger. You're still in control, but you are really feeling agitated. When you are upset, your behaviors are likely to include letting others know you are struggling intensely with your angry feelings. You are ruminating and rehearsing arguments over and over.

Furious (extreme)

This is when you feel maxed-out on your anger gauge. You are feeling your bodily reactions very strongly, like you're about to spin out of control, and you want to retaliate in a mean way. Your furious behaviors may include yelling, talking over others, or feeling like you can't hear anything else due to your own angry thoughts.

Now let's take what you have learned about anger and go to school with it to learn some tools to manage it there.

MINDFULNESS FOR SCHOOL ANGER

Do you ever find yourself feeling irritated, annoyed, or even furious about situations and pressures at school or when doing your homework after school? Sometimes anger-provoking school situations can get in the way of getting things done in terms of the many demands and responsibilities that come your way. When this occurs, mindfulness can guide you to cope in more appropriate ways. The more you can identify what these situations are, the better you will be able to understand them and cope with them.

SCHOOL ANGER

Sit comfortably or lie down and close your eyes to reflect on occasions when you felt angry about something at school. To help get in touch with these thoughts and feelings, consider tough classes, demanding teachers, academic frustrations, and other disappointments or upsetting situations related to academic demands. Just notice your related thoughts and feelings toward these or other stressful academic pressures, without judging or reacting to them.

What academic-related situations lead you to feel anger?

_____

_____

What negative and self-sabotaging thoughts come to mind?

_____

_____

What do you notice in your body about how it responds to the anger you feel about school demands?

_____

_____

How does your anger about school affect your ability to do your schoolwork?

_____

_____

How does noticing your angry thoughts and feelings about school-related anger help you to let them go?

_____

_____

How have you successfully managed school anger in the past?

_____

_____

BREATHING OUT SCHOOL ANGER

Imagine a past situation at school that you became angry about. Keeping your anger thermometer in mind, were you irritated, upset, or furious? Now, holding on to this memory, calmly breathe in. As you breathe out, imagine your school-related anger leaving your body. For maximum effect, silently remind yourself that you're breathing in and out, and tell yourself what you are trying to achieve in a few simple statements. Here is a sample of what you can say to yourself while doing this exercise:

Breathing in, I am feeling calmer.
Breathing out, I am releasing my frustration and anger toward school.
Breathing in, I breathe in new energy.
Breathing out, I release stressful school frustrations.

How did this breathing exercise feel for you?

_____

_____

What was it like to release your school anger through your breath?

_____

_____

How can focusing on your breath in the present moment gently help you shift away from anger to a calmer state at school?

_____

_____

How might you feel and behave differently in the face of school frustrations by breathing out and letting go of angry feelings?

_____

_____

RELEASING SCHOOL ANGER
THROUGH THE CLOUD

Being angry can really leave you feeling weighed down and restricted. Here is a mindful activity to help you feel freed up as you watch your angry feelings about school float away.

Reflect for a few minutes on a range of angry feelings you may have about school. Write one or more of those stressors on the cloud. As you breathe in, reflect on these school stressors and imagine them waiting to be released. As you breathe out, imagine the outer cloud border as a medium through which your stressors can flow into the surrounding air. Repeat this a few times.

How did it feel to let your school-related stressors gather in the cloud?

_____

_____

_____

What was it like to release them into the surrounding air?

_____

_____

_____

Why does letting go of school anger, instead of holding on to it, help you feel less burdened by it?

_____

_____

_____

How can letting go of anger help you to be more successful at school?

_____

_____

_____

FINDING
SCHOOL SERENITY

When schoolwork frustrations are getting the best of you and you're feeling irritated, annoyed, or even furious because of something like being lost while you're doing your homework, finding some what I call "Seconds of Serenity" can help you calm down.

Imagine sitting on top of a hill near a highway and watching the cars go by. Or imagine looking down on railroad cars moving along a track that stretches in each direction as far as you can see. As you see the cars go by, think of them as your angry thoughts, and just notice them as they pass. If an angry thought seems to appear over and over again, or it just won't pass, then say to yourself, "I accept that this anger is what I am thinking about right now, and that's okay."

How does a quick, calming letting-go image as presented in this activity serve to give you a quick and easy coping skill for school anger?

_____

_____

_____

If you were to learn to let go of school anger with Seconds of Serenity, what would be the obvious and not-so-obvious benefits for you?

_____

_____

_____

How can more easily finding serenity build on itself over time to make it easier to access when you quickly need it when facing school demands?

_____

_____

_____

MINDFULLY MANAGING
TEST FRUSTRATIONS

Have you had the experience of feeling well prepared for a test, only to begin and soon feel like your teacher is unfairly presenting you with material you have not had a chance to master? Or perhaps the test is emphasizing a part of what you studied that seems less relevant than what you think is important. Maybe you think the test's content or structure is altogether unfair. Perhaps you start to feel angry at yourself or your teacher or both. In these situations, keeping your cool may actually help you get a better grade.

Here are two quick mindfulness practices to calm down your anger and get you focused back on your quiz or test:

Breathing in Calming Confidence to Conquer Frustration

You can do this exercise proactively or in response to the first sign of frustration you feel when taking a test. This sign may be your mind racing or tension in your face, jaw, hands, or chest.

Gently breathe in while picturing all your hard work and knowledge filling your mind. Now breathe out any feelings of frustration and anger. Do this three times.

Feeling Your Feet on the Floor

A common response to feeling frustration and anger is to feel agitated and restless in your body. Grounding yourself by resettling your feet on the floor can help you establish feelings of being centered and back in control.

Take a few relaxing breaths, and while doing so notice the feeling of security you gain by replanting your feet on the floor. Notice that you are here, present, and ready to give this test your best effort.

How can having these two quick tools above give you added confidence and help you focus when taking future tests?

_____

What are some quizzes or tests you took in the past where managing your frustration and anger may have helped you do better on them?

_____

What could prevent you from using these tools?

_____

How can you overcome any obstacles to practicing these test-centering skills of quickly focusing on your breath and feeling your feet to feel calmer?

_____

CBT FOR SCHOOL ANGER

Cognitive behavioral therapy helps you understand your school-related anger by helping you focus on how to identify, challenge, and respond to angry thoughts about situations going on. Managing your thoughts, feelings, and actions related to school will go a long way toward keeping anger from getting in the way of your performance.

CBT emphasizes changing thoughts and feelings in order to alter behaviors. At the same time, changing how you behave and how you approach your school responsibilities can also help your attitude and feelings about school. Acting differently can lead to some healthier thoughts and feelings to get you back on top of your school challenges.

As depicted in the graphic below, negative thinking (e.g., "I'll never be able to learn this!") and negative feelings (e.g., frustration, hopelessness) are the source of much school-related anger. This leads to negative actions (e.g., shutting down and avoiding schoolwork). What results is a self-feeding cycle of school anxiety, as illustrated in the graphic below. Notice the cyclical connection of angry thoughts, feelings, and behaviors.

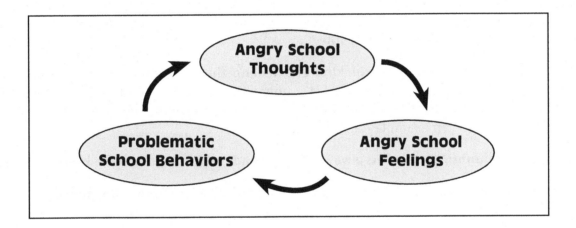

STAYING
COOL WITH HOMEWORK

Let's look at how anger impacts Liz, a junior in high school. Liz loves being on the cheerleading squad, but it takes a lot of time, making it even more challenging for her to keep up with her homework. Liz gets really upset when her teachers give way-y-y too much homework, given the busy schedule she has going on. Making things even more stressful, she has loaded herself with honors and AP classes. Liz works hard, trying to maintain an A average as much as possible.

When the difficulty of Liz's homework ramps up, it is intensified due to her habit of distorting her thinking to believe that her teachers are trying to make her miserable. She has noticed lately on her anger meter that she is feeling increasingly upset. Having counterproductively taken her frustrations out on her parents and siblings, Liz also feels like just shutting down. She is now aware of even more escalating thoughts of blaming her teachers for making her life horrible.

What might Liz be distortedly thinking and feeling that is leading her to feel angrier? Check out the prompts below for Liz's unhealthy thoughts, and suggest healthier thoughts for her. (The first unhelpful thought and healthier alternative thought are provided for you as an example for this activity.)

Unhelpful thought: "My teachers always pile it on and make it impossible to keep up."

Instead Liz can think: "My teachers really want me to learn this important material."

Unhelpful thought: "I hate doing homework—it sucks!"

Instead Liz can think: _____.

Unhelpful thought: "Everyone else has an easier time than I do getting this done!"

Instead Liz can think: _____.

In referring back to the basic types of cognitive distortions described on page 36, which ones were represented by Liz's unhelpful thoughts?

_____

How can managing her angry thoughts and feelings help Liz become more productive at school?

_____

LOWERING SCHOOL ANGER BY
LOSING NEGATIVE LABELS

Have you ever given yourself a negative label that ends up feeding your frustrations and leading to anger that interferes with your schoolwork? Some common negative labels teens may put on themselves include "lazy," "stupid," "dumb," "incompetent," or "less than."

Check out the negative self-labels shown below, and provide a more reasonable alternative to them in each blank. The first two are examples to help you to complete the exercise.

Lazy vs. *motivationally blocked*

Learning disabled vs. *challenged at learning certain things*

No good at school vs. _____

Stupid vs. _____

Failure vs. _____

Incompetent vs. _____

Less than vs. _____

Careless vs. _____

Can't vs. _____

Spacy vs. _____

How can negative self-labels related to school get in the way of your schoolwork?

_____

_____

Do you have peers whom you have observed being really hard on themselves by referring to themselves with negative labels? Why might they do this?

_____

_____

What do you observe happening to the motivation of others who trash themselves with negative labels?

_____

_____

MANAGING
MATH ANGER

Dave, a junior in high school, found himself agonizing and feeling super frustrated over his math-related struggles. He had persistent fears of "becoming a failure," which were especially triggered when he would try to do his math homework. Once he got past negatively labeling himself as a "total failure" and unfavorably comparing himself to others who were better in math, he realized he needed outside help to perform better.

By identifying that he had a problem grasping math concepts, and no longer being solely consumed by beating himself up, he sought outside help to get through his math struggles.

Put a check mark next to each healthy coping statement below that Dave may have used to stay calm and seek help:

_____ Just because math is hard for me does not mean I am a failure.

_____ Many struggle with math when learning new material.

_____ Just because math comes more easily to others does not mean I can't do it, too.

_____ Getting help doing this is a lot smarter than stewing and not doing anything about it.

_____ Reflecting on how I got through some other hard times with math gives me confidence now.

_____ It may take me longer, but that is better than going fast and making careless mistakes.

_____ Even if this test does not go well, I know that I'll give it my best shot.

WEIGH THE EVIDENCE TO
STOP ANGER

CBT helps you identify and weigh the evidence for the distorted thoughts that drive your anger. The following exercise will help you reflect on situations at school where you feel angry and then look for the evidence (or lack of it) to support these thoughts.

First, identify three school-related angry thoughts:

1._____.

2._____.

3. _____.

Now answer the following questions about each of the thoughts you've listed above:

Is this thought based on facts or feelings?

_____

_____

What feelings result from being in these situations and saying these unhealthy statements about yourself?

_____

_____

What are some healthy alternative thoughts to your angry ones?

_____

_____

How can recognizing others' anger about school help you see it in yourself?

_____

_____

How can seeing other helpful, alternative ways that peers better manage their school-related anger help you to spot and manage yours better as well?

_____

_____

EMOTIONAL SMARTS
FOR BETTER LEARNING

What if working smarter will help you do well with less effort? The more you can manage your anger effectively at school, the smarter you will feel by being better able to focus, persist through challenges, and make meaningful progress. Explore the following tool to see the importance of working smarter vs. just harder.

To further understand how managing your thoughts, feelings, and actions can create or reduce your angry feelings about school, consider these questions:

What are some triggering situations you encounter, such as overwhelming school assignments, that lead you to think counterproductively when doing your work?

_____

_____

Which distorted thought patterns (refer to the list on page 36) most often lead you to feel angry about school demands?

_____

_____

Describe the links among your anger-related thoughts, feelings, and behaviors that sabotage your school motivation.

_____

_____

How does thinking like a perfectionistic lead to procrastination and then anger?

_____

_____

What is a school-related setback you became angry about that you can now reframe with self-supporting and motivating thoughts?

_____

_____

DOES YOUR TEACHER
TRIGGER YOUR ANGER?

Struggling with a teacher at school can set a negative tone for you in many ways and lead to feelings of frustration, resentment, and anger. Teachers face many pressures, including being responsible to cover class material, manage classroom dynamics, and support students in need. They are human just like you. If a teacher interacts with you in a way that triggers some negative underlying feelings, you may feel angry.

Check out the following sequence of trigger, thought, feeling, and behavior in response to a student's unfavorable interaction with his teacher.

Trigger: A teacher tells a student that he should have read over the lesson after the student answers a question incorrectly.

Thought: *"I hate this teacher. All he does is embarrass me. He should know that I'm really trying but just can't seem to grasp this material."*

Feeling: Frustrated over not being able to answer the question, embarrassed, humiliated, hopeless, angry!

Behavior: Shuts down and tunes out the teacher.

Put a check mark next to the cognitive distortions that the teen experienced in this example.

____ All-or-Nothing Thinking   ____ Should Thinking

____ Jumping to Conclusions   ____ Negative Labeling

____ Negative Filtering   ____ Negative Comparisons

____ Catastrophizing

What are some alternative thoughts to dispute this student's thought distortion(s)?

_____

_____

How could the student have challenged his upsetting thoughts toward this teacher to help him feel better about his teacher and approach him to discuss what is going on?

_____

_____

GETTING GRATEFUL AND
RELEASING SCHOOL ANGER

Positive psychology encourages striving to focus with gratitude on what is going well in school, which diminishes anger. When you bring gratitude into the way you view school-related stressors, your anger diminishes.

Take a few gentle, deep breaths in through your nose, down to your stomach, and out through your mouth. While doing so, reflect on the things that you appreciate about school. Below are some guiding prompts to help you focus your thoughts.

Who is a teacher or other staff member at your school whom you value seeing every day?

_____

_____

_____

What is it about this person that you appreciate?

_____

_____

_____

What class or classes do you appreciate as having been positive experiences for you?

_____

_____

_____

What are you grateful about accomplishing at school recently? How can connecting with this accomplishment calm you down when you are struggling in the future?

_____

_____

_____

SCHOOL ANGER

While you may be more familiar with the word rap in reference to music, in this case consider another meaning for RAP—Responsible Anger Replacement. Substituting a positive, goal-driven behavior when you are angry can help you feel less frustrated, less angry, and more productive. This is another way of managing your emotions, which leaves you working smarter. Many smart students don't work smart, and many students who struggle with learning concepts could learn better if they approached school demands in smart ways to help them gain success.

Responsible anger replacement for school can take the following format:

As an alternative to _____ (negative coping strategy),

instead I will _____ (positive action).

Take a few moments and reflect on the list below to get some ideas of positive, goal-driven behaviors you can use for anger about school concerns:

- Apply "I'll Do It Anyway" (see page 43).

- Set aside time to study.

- Review the parts you understand.

- Ask a peer for help.

- Speak to your teacher or school counselor.

- Make an outline for a written project.

- Break complex projects down into smaller, workable parts.

- Set a timer to do a project.

- Take a break when you feel frustrated.

- Keep realistic expectations about the time that is needed.

- Be optimistic where possible.

- Get better sleep.

- Write down assignments properly.

- Own your learning by thinking critically.

- Check over notes for understanding, and ask a friend or teacher if something is unclear.

- Keep electronic devices on silent and out of reach when you need to concentrate.

- Make up a schedule for when to do your homework.

- Ask for help when it's needed.

Look at the following sentences containing negative ways of handling anger, and replace them with positive alternatives from the list that may work for you.

Instead of telling myself my teacher is stupid when I feel stuck on homework, I will:

_____

_____.

Instead of continuing to put off starting this English paper, I will:

_____

_____.

Instead of swearing when I get a math problem wrong, I will:

_____

_____.

Instead of complaining and whining about how difficult an assignment is, I will:

_____

_____.

Instead of blaming myself for not being able to understand the assignment, I will:

_____

_____.

Instead of letting my frustration influence me to rush through this assignment and make careless errors, I will:

_____

_____.

Instead of expecting to fail or fall short, I will:

_____

_____.

How can implementing these specific actions help lower your anger over school demands?

_____

_____

_____

When facing school demands, why do we sometimes fail to do what makes our lives easier?

_____

_____

_____

What can you do to remind yourself to work smarter at school?

_____

_____

_____

GETTING GRITTY

You may think that being super smart is what makes people successful. Yet according to important research conducted by University of Pennsylvania psychologist Angela Duckworth, a huge predictor of what helps you achieve success is grit. *Grit,* as we have mentioned earlier, is your ability to persist and bounce back from setbacks as you pursue your goals. When it comes to managing school frustrations, grit empowers you to put yourself out there and strive toward reasonable goals (not unrealistic ones) as you face challenges. If you've ever heard the fable about the tortoise and the hare, then you already know about the great things you can achieve by having grit. In that fable, the tortoise and the hare are in a race. The hare sprints ahead but stops midway to take a nap, and ends up losing the race to the slow but persistent tortoise. It is the slow tortoise's persistence, otherwise known as grit, that helps him win the race—even when the initial challenge looked overwhelming.

As an example of someone who persisted in the face of challenges, consider the author J. K. Rowling. She personifies grit. Her manuscript for the first Harry Potter book was rejected a dozen times. Have you ever noticed that when you overcome a stressful school challenge, you feel stronger? Keeping that in mind can help you persevere, even if there's a chance you may fall short or fail altogether.

You can inspire your own grit for school by taking to heart the philosophy that you can achieve successes, both big and small, through dedication and effort. Even if you initially fail to reach an academic goal, you can continue studying or doing whatever it is that might eventually get you there. What's really cool is that your brain will grow as you adapt to this new and different path toward your objective.

GETTING GRITTY AND
WRITING OFF ANGER

Please recall or reread the section "A Special Note about Procrastination" (page 41) as you consider this goal-oriented approach for the following situation, which most students can identify with.

You have a paper due for English class soon and you have been avoiding it for quite some time. You just saw the teacher in the hallway, which made your stomach start doing flips. On the bus ride home, you feel overwhelmed and angry about having to get the paper done.

Below is a list of positive coping behaviors to get you moving in a gritty direction. Put a check mark next to each one you could use to cope in this situation:

_____ Clean out your backpack or do some mindless task to stop stewing and get into doing.

_____ Realize that motivation for the paper will come once you begin it.

_____ Put your cell phone out of sight in case it buzzes or lights up with a message.

_____ Develop a doable set of subgoals for the paper, including selecting a topic, gathering sources, writing an outline, and committing to getting it done by a certain time.

_____ Give yourself credit for showing some grit when you work through your previous resistance and begin to actively engage.

_____ Begin a short initial work session to make starting the paper less anxiety-provoking, and then feel how your resistance is broken.

_____ Get into flow by reconnecting with your intention and sense of purpose for doing the paper.

_____ To feel motivated, feel positive about the benefits of completing the task. It may be hard to believe, but there's tons more benefit to getting this project done than just getting it out of your hair.

BECOME SUCCESSFUL
IN SCHOOL

Let's now look at optimism as a way to help you become less frustrated and more successful in school. Reflect on a time when filling yourself with negative thoughts led you to feel angry about a school assignment.

What were some pessimistic things you said to yourself that led you to feel angry?

_____

_____

_____

What were some other feelings you had that accompanied your anger?

_____

_____

_____

How can reminding yourself to know your value help you feel better about getting through challenging school tasks?

_____

_____

_____

How can having grit to push through demanding work leave you feeling more optimistic about it afterward?

_____

_____

_____

How can optimism become "the gift that keeps on giving" to help you ward off self-sabotaging anger about school?

_____

_____

_____

LEARNING WITH
POSITIVE ENERGY

Have you noticed that when you are mentally into learning in your difficult classes you have fewer negative feelings about it? Ask yourself the following questions to get connected to the class and to disconnect from angry feelings about being there.

How does learning this material challenge me for the better?

_____

_____

_____

How will I feel after embracing the challenge of learning this material?

_____

_____

_____

How can this teacher's effort inspire me to feel more tuned in to what they are sharing with me right now?

_____

_____

_____

How does learning in this class help me to learn other things that may not be as easy to learn?

_____

_____

_____

LEARNING TO
LET IT GO

Mindfulness can help you defuse anger in social situations by observing angry thoughts without judging them or immediately reacting to them. The more you learn to observe your thoughts without needing to act on them, the freer you may feel to see choices in how you can effectively handle peers in difficult situations. Thinking of your thoughts as bubbles floating above you can help you watch your angry thoughts and let them go.

1. Find a quiet, safe place where you can lie down, get comfortable, and take a few mindful, relaxing breaths.

2. Now gently reflect on a social situation you have been angry about, are angry about, or could become angry about in the future.

3. Imagine this social situation you are angry about flowing from within you, out of you, and up as an angry thought-filled bubble that now gently moves away from you.

4. Watch the bubble containing these thoughts as it aimlessly moves about, and then watch it drift away. You may want to visualize it popping as well.

5. Let your mind flow with related angry thoughts and picture these similarly as taking the form of bubbles flowing out of you and joining in a stream of other angry thought bubbles leaving you and floating away.

6. Repeat steps 1-5 until your angry thoughts are no longer surfacing.

7. Finish by taking a deep breath and exhaling slowly.

How did visualizing your angry thoughts about a social situation as a bubble help you to let it go?

_____

How does seeing your anger as leaving you give you a sense of distance from it and serenity?

_____

How can letting go of socially-related anger help you engage or reengage peers with whom you felt negative energy?

_____

In what social settings and potential situations would it be helpful to stay mindful of this tool for possible use in the future?

_____

MINDFUL COMMUNICATION FOR MANAGING ANGER

Your connections with others will be smoother and have less conflict if you engage them mindfully. Being mindful when you have conversations with your peers and others means being as present as you can when you communicate. This lowers the likelihood of saying things impulsively or without thought, which could result in unintended conflicts and misunderstandings, which, in turn, could provoke anger.

The main elements for mindful communication are listening closely without judgment, speaking clearly, and being honest. How great would you feel if your friends listened to you as if you were a celebrity whom they admired and respected? You would likely treasure that experience. In contrast, have you ever caught yourself during a conversation being more concerned with what you were going to say next, rather than listening to what the other person is saying now? How about that "ouch feeling" when the other person realized that you had been spacing out and not really listening? Rest assured that this happens to all of us at times. Let's work on mindful listening—a challenge for all of us.

MOVING INTO
MINDFUL LISTENING

You can arrange to do this activity with a friend and practice it while conversing with them, or just imagine that you're having a conversation with this person.

Take a few breaths and reflect on your intention to really listen. Next, listen attentively without judgment. Maintain good eye contact without interrupting your friend. When they pause for you to respond, remember that your tone and body language count. Lean in slightly without slouching; be kind in your tone; maintain solid, supportive eye contact; and say "mm-hmm" or nod to show agreement. These little things go a long way toward mindful listening. This caring, mindful awareness will help you better listen to your friend's words. Notice how mindful listening feels and whether your friend seems to appreciate it.

Did listening mindfully leave you feeling more connected?

_____

_____

_____

Can you see how mindful listening helps you more accurately understand others and communicates that you care?

_____

_____

_____

Can you see how listening mindfully creates less work in understanding and feeling closer to others—and how it lowers the likelihood of misunderstandings?

_____

_____

_____

MINDFUL SPEAKING

Now that you've practiced mindful listening, it is time to focus on speaking mindfully. Mindful speaking is all about being aware of how the feelings and thoughts you express affect others and reflect upon you. This "Ready, Set, Go" intention (presented in the section on mindful messaging) keeps you from stepping into the social bear-trap of speaking impulsively.

By being aware of how you express your thoughts and feelings, you will less likely rush in to interrupt and say what you don't really mean, or just babble on. Keep in mind that in our fast-paced, distracted world, speaking mindfully can be challenging. Interrupting or rambling is something everyone does—but if we bring mindful attention to our speaking, it happens less often. And when it does happen, we can catch ourselves and adjust, bringing our words back to mindful speech.

SETTING YOURSELF UP FOR
MINDFUL SPEAKING

As with the mindful listening exercise, you can arrange to do this with a friend, practice it during a conversation with them, or just do it in your imagination.

Take a few breaths and reflect on your intention to really listen. When it is your time to respond to what your friend has said, take a few deep, calming breaths as you gently notice, without judgment, how you are thinking and feeling. Express yourself openly (within reason), and if there is conflict, try to avoid reacting by blaming (shifting the conflict entirely onto your friend), criticizing (throwing out negative comments that shut down your friend from speaking), or using judgmental words (implying that your friend is below you).

How did mindful speaking work for you, and how did your friend respond?

_____

_____

_____

Did you feel more or less in control of how you expressed yourself and what you said?

_____

_____

_____

What are some past situations with others that led to anger and may have gone better if you had spoken in a more mindful manner?

_____

_____

_____

What can get in the way of mindful speaking, and how can you avoid these obstacles?

_____

_____

_____

MINDFULNESS FOR PEER CONFLICT

We have so far addressed ways to understand, build, and strengthen friendships in a proactive manner. But what about when you and your friends suddenly find yourself in Conflict City without knowing how to get out? Let's navigate out of there by managing peer conflicts with mindfulness.

Most people, even those who claim to thrive on drama, don't really like conflict. Conflicts with peers can create big-time anxiety. But conflict, whether spoken or unspoken, is inevitable. When it happens, you may worry about how big it will get, how long it will last, how widely it will spread, and what potential gossip can arise from it.

LETTING GO

A PEER CONFLICT

The acronym NOW can help you bring in intention, attention, and attitude for practicing mindfulness. NOW stands for:

N: <u>N</u>oticing what is around you.

O: <u>O</u>bserving by opening up your curiosity.

W: <u>W</u>illingly letting go of unhelpful, distracting thoughts and feelings.

Take three centering, calming breaths. Think about the types of conflicts you have with friends—conflicts that trigger upsetting feelings for you.

Notice: Reflect on a past conflict with a friend, or imagine having a conflict, and notice how you are feeling and what is upsetting you.

Observe (Open Up Your Curiosity): Observe the interaction and conflict by imagining that you are looking down on the scene from above. Picture yourself floating on the ceiling, looking down at both you and your friend. If the conflict occurred through text messages or social media, notice your thoughts and feelings about that as well. Observe your reactions about the conflict without judgment.

Willingly Let Go: Release the conflict by giving yourself a little coaching, telling yourself that you will just feel worse if you continue to dwell on it or magnify it. Reflect on your strength to rise above this conflict as a tolerant, forgiving friend.

How can moving to NOW when having a conflict with someone give you the emotional space to pause and slow down your racing mind and realize that you don't have to react out of anger?

_____

_____

Can you see how the next time that you have a conflict or argument with a friend, mindfully practicing NOW can help you let go of the conflict?

_____

_____

What can you do to be more ready to use NOW the next time an upsetting situation with a friend arises?

_____

_____

MANAGING ANGER IN CLOSE RELATIONSHIPS

Next, let's discuss an aspect of life where angry emotions can bubble up quickly and become overwhelming—dating and relationships.

For example, could there be, or has there been, a situation where your significant other behaved less than trustfully—and could there be, or have there been, ways in which you reacted less than respectfully to their behavior? Or vice versa: maybe it was you who didn't trust your partner, and your partner reacted too harshly. Seeing all this—and just seeing it, without judging it—allows you to think about how your instinctive reactions compare to how you would *like* to respond. Mindfulness in loving relationships helps you notice your thoughts and feelings without overreacting. This can help minimize conflicts, giving you less to feel angry about.

MANAGING ANGER IN AN
INTIMATE RELATIONSHIP

Begin by taking a few calming breaths and picturing yourself in a heated moment with your significant other.

Reflect on how you feel hurt and/or angry. Now imagine observing these thoughts and emotions without getting caught up in them. By noticing these feelings without judging them, you can regain a sense of your emotional balance.

Can you see how mindfulness helps you lower your anger and experience your relationship in a calmer way?

_____

_____

_____

Do you think that rehearsing how to handle conflicts in your relationship could be useful for managing your anger?

_____

_____

_____

To wrap up this tool, be mindful that trust promotes calmer feelings. Put a check mark next to each way to build trust in your current relationship or the next one you are in:

_____ Having respect when communicating with the other person (whether face-to-face or through text).

_____ Being okay with each of you spending time alone.

_____ Being able to spend time with friends outside of your relationship.

_____ Not jumping to conclusions about the other person's behavior when you feel doubt.

_____ Treating the other person as a friend.

_____ Being proud of who you each are as individuals and as a couple.

_____ Speaking and listening to the other person in a caring, emotionally-safe way.

CBT FOR SOCIAL ANGER

CBT helps you challenge the kind of thinking that leaves you smoldering with anger on the inside or blowing up on the outside as a result of things that occur in your relationships with others. CBT can help you consider what you think is super important for controlling your anger in social situations.

By changing how your think, feel, and respond, you will be able to control the anger that you experience with others. One word that is a huge culprit in driving anger is *hate*. Let's find a way to manage this troublesome word with some CBT.

REFRAMING HATE

AS DISLIKE

Consistent with the CBT model, changing your self-talk from hate to dislike can help you manage your anger. When you think or say the word *hate*, it inflames your reactive brain. As an alternative, try saying or thinking *dislike*, a milder word that helps to calm down your reactive brain.

Consider the following socially-related examples:

"I hate it when he says that!" vs. "I dislike when he says that."

"I hate being left out of that group!" vs. "I dislike being left out of that group."

"I hate how selfish he is!" vs. "I dislike how selfish he is."

Now try to complete some on your own.

I hate _____ vs. I dislike _____

I hate _____ vs. I dislike _____

I hate _____ vs. I dislike _____

I hate _____ vs. I dislike _____

I hate _____ vs. I dislike _____

STOP "SHOULDING"

ON OTHERS

Another problematic word leading to angry thoughts and feelings is *should*. If you recall, "should thinking" is one of the cognitive distortions we discussed earlier.

Let's take a more in-depth look at what happens to your social relationships when you "should" all over them. By *shoulding* I am referring to how we can knowingly or unknowingly impose rigid expectations on others, resulting in our feeling angry toward them.

Reflect for a few minutes about people, times, and places where you think and say the word *should*, which could spark or heighten existing conflicts. Now see if any of these statements approximate some of your own anger-triggering past, current, or potentially future shoulds. Put a check mark next to each statement that closely fits for you. (Note some blank lines are available as prompts to add your own should statements—not that you should.)

____ They shouldn't have said that.   ____ I shouldn't have to wait for you.

____ He should know better.   ____ You should understand how I feel.

____ I shouldn't even care.   ____ You should do something about it.

____ You shouldn't feel that way.   ____ You shouldn't have done that.

You should _____.

He should _____.

She shouldn't _____.

We shouldn't _____.

Now try substituting the phrase "I would like" instead of "should" in each of the above examples.

How does thinking and saying *should* in your social interactions lead you to have more conflicts?

_____

How does thinking and saying *should* when interacting with others create obstacles instead of building connections?

_____

How does it feel to replace your *should* thoughts and verbalizations with a less aggressive statement such as, "I would like . . ."?

_____

HOW WILL MY
ANGER IMPACT ME LATER

In the true spirit of CBT, looking at the potential behavioral consequences of our anger can help us proactively manage our thoughts and the underlying feelings that drive us to it. Below is a magic seven-word question to promote anger management by thinking ahead.

This seven-word question—**"How will my anger impact me later?"**—is your powerful formula for proactively managing anger.

Reflect on a situation where your anger made it worse by you impulsively engaging in behaviors that were destructive. Check the following if any of these angry actions played a role.

____ You yelled

____ You interrupted

____ You wrote someone off

____ You bullied

____ You gave up

____ You lost trust

____ You shut down and said nothing

____ You made a rash, poor decision

____ You were defensive

____ You lost sight of the actual concern

____ You impulsively judged someone negatively

Let's consider an example of how, by not thinking about the impact of her actions, Anita got in trouble:

José tells his girlfriend Anita that he will text her when he gets home from football practice. Anita waits for José's text at the anticipated time, but he does not send a message as she expected he would. Thinking that she is being dissed and feeling upset, she further thinks, "See, I knew he'd be a jerk, just like every other guy!" Thinking that José is a jerk makes Anita feel she deserves to be angry.

Now let's stop Anita's anger stream from flowing any further by empowering her to consider how she will feel afterward if she just reactively gets more upset. Two initial examples are provided. Can you fill in the remaining blanks with other helpful coping thoughts for Anita?

For example, she might say to herself, "Maybe José got busy at home," or "He does get forgetful at times, so maybe it is best to chill out and give him a little more time."

_____

_____.

WHEN SOCIAL SHAME FEELS EXPLOSIVE

Sophia, age 17, was a high school senior who had a mad crush on Candace, a girl in her class. Candace had recently broken up with her boyfriend. Candace saw Sophia as a "sort-of friend," but did not have the same feelings for her. Sophia texted Candace one day and asked her if she'd like to go out on a date. Candace took a screenshot of the text exchange and sent it to a trusted friend—who then sent it to other people.

When Sophia heard about this from a mutual friend, she felt totally humiliated and furious. At the same time, she had a habit of pleasing people and really did not want to lose Candace as a friend. She immediately spoke to Candace at school, and Candace tried to convince her that she was "just kidding around" and that what she did was not a big deal. Sophia asked Candace if she was sorry for what she did. Candace said that she was sorry in what seemed like a shallow way, but felt that Sophia was more upset than she should be.

Over the next few weeks, Sophia felt a reemergence of her feelings of embarrassment and shame, and now was furious. Feeling her head pounding and her stomach tighten when she saw Candace in the hallway, she went up and got in her face, cornering her right up against her locker. A crowd gathered, and Candace, who this time was really trying to apologize, was not being heard by Sophia, who was enraged. A teacher walking by promptly dispersed the crowd and took both Candace and Sophia to the office of the school counselor (who was skilled in CBT), where they were able to explore their thoughts, feelings, and behaviors and talk it out. It helped Sophia that Candace readily conceded that what she did was impulsive, reckless, and humiliating. She further apologized to Sophia in a more heartfelt way. Let's take a closer look at how Sophia could have used her CBT skills to help her get through this tough time.

HEALTHY COPING STATEMENTS

During her meeting with the counselor, Sophia was guided to reframe her prevailing thought that "My life is ruined!" to the following more rational and helpful thoughts:

- "I know my value, and that is what is most important."

- "My life may have felt like it was ruined at the moment, but when I consider all those who do care about me, I have a lot to feel good about."

- "Handling something this upsetting makes me a stronger person."

- "If all this pain helped Candace to learn something valuable about respecting others, then that is something else I can feel good about."

- "Even if Candace is not into me in a romantic way, I can feel good that I took the risk of letting her know how I felt."

Can you fill in the blank lines below by writing in your own suggestions of some more rational, helpful thoughts for Sophia to use in coping with this difficult situation?

_____

_____

_____

_____

_____.

Deciding to End an Intimate Relationship

What is the healthy thing to do if the intimate relationship you are in is no longer satisfying? You may be worried that your partner's anger could erupt at the end of a relationship. Maybe you feel this would be fueled by anxiety about being the center of gossipy attention, especially if the rumor mill churns out unfavorable or unsavory stories about your breakup. Even though breakups can be difficult, you may find that being free of the struggles of a relationship that was not satisfying can bring you a strong sense of relief.

The way you think about ending a relationship is important. It also really helps if you see *all* relationships as learning experiences. The less you see a breakup as a flop or a failure, the more you can see it as an opportunity to be grateful for your openness to connecting with someone you valued in a deep, special way. Relationships that end can help you understand yourself better, too—for example, they can help you determine the degree to which you value "together time" vs. "alone time," or the level of independence vs. sense of commitment that feels manageable to you.

If you find yourself wanting to move out of your relationship, be open, honest, and respectful in doing so. The old standby line "I just need space," especially if you have an attraction to someone else, can feel misleading to the person you want to end the relationship with. And breaking up by suddenly not responding to someone's text messages or by texting that person "I can't see you anymore" is even more cruel. For helping to manage your own feelings and preventing unnecessary anger in your significant other, taking the high road and keeping any possible negative feelings under control is the way to go.

COPING WITH
UNREASONABLE ANGER

Let's look at how CBT can help you cope when someone is seemingly unreasonably angry at you, no matter what the circumstances may be related to. Clearly, it is important for you to own any of your actions that may hurt or offend others. That said, if someone appears angry with you and you can't work through it, then keeping your cool can really help you cope.

Put a check mark next to each coping statement that can help you stay centered if someone expresses anger at you:

_____ Just because someone expresses anger at me does not mean I did something wrong.

_____ If someone is angry at me, it may be true that I said or did something that they interpreted as threatening or upsetting.

_____ I am not responsible for others' feelings.

_____ I am responsible to try to treat other people in a respectful way.

_____ Saying "I'm sorry" is a helpful way to heal a conflict, but showing insight and trying to understand what the other person's thoughts and feelings were is better than blindly saying, "I'm sorry."

_____ When someone gets angry, the way they handle it is a gauge of their maturity.

_____ Anger is a healthy emotion, but there are healthy and unhealthy ways to express it.

Write in some additional coping statements you can reflect on in order to stay grounded when "over-the-top" anger arises in someone you have a relationship with.

_____

_____

_____

POSITIVE PSYCHOLOGY FOR SOCIAL ANGER

When social pressures arise, it is easy to lose sight of your talents, qualities, and accomplishments that you can use to feel calmer in anger-provoking social situations. Gratitude can also help you find your way out of feeling awkward, lost, and angry in challenging times with peers.

As an example of reconnecting with your strengths when you feel stressed with anger, let's turn to a situation that happened with Ilana when her emotions reached an almost furious level. Ilana was struggling socially in school, where many of her female peers were competing ruthlessly for popularity. They gossiped nonstop and, at times, were really mean to one another. One day, things really got stressful for Ilana when a girl whom she had just started to open up to was giving her the cold shoulder. She felt very empty inside, reflecting on past friends who had disappointed and abandoned her. That night she messaged another friend, Carly, saying that her life was going really badly, and she confided that out of frustration she had intentionally hurt herself by cutting her arm.

Carly, wanting to be supportive of Ilana, and knowing the dangers of self-harming behavior, sensed that it was important to get further help for her. So the next day, Carly spoke to a school counselor. When Ilana was summoned to see the school counselor and learned the reason why, she was initially hurt and disappointed with Carly, fuming, "I can't believe she went behind my back. She's just like the other girls."

Fortunately, the school counselor, by being a patient and supportive listener, helped Ilana see that Carly was a true friend for caring about her. To de-escalate her anger, the school counselor used tools from positive psychology and encouraged Ilana to consider her own strengths that she had lost sight of, and also helped her identify some strengths she didn't know she possessed. Together, Ilana and her counselor made a list of her strengths:

- authenticity and openness with others
- kindness
- commitment and loyalty
- creativity
- humor
- nonjudgmental

Ilana found it really calming to make this list that helped her see her worth. It felt freeing from all the pressures she'd been feeling, because no matter what anyone—such as the gossipy girls in her grade—said or did, she felt okay about herself as a person having many good qualities and as a loyal, caring friend to a lucky few. Ilana initially had little sense of her own strengths, but her school counselor did a great job helping her become aware of them. Her experience teaches us a valuable lesson that noticing the good that others see in us can help us rediscover our own value when we're struggling with our self-worth.

The following tool will help you see your strengths through the eyes of the important people in your life. Once you allow yourself to reflect on the strengths others see in you, you'll likely start to perceive other strengths you possess. Your stream of personal strengths may start to flow slowly, but if you can be a little patient, it'll then likely move along more abundantly.

CALMING YOURSELF

WITH YOUR STRENGTHS

Ask someone you feel close to and trust (e.g., a friend, a family member, or a teacher) what they value about you. If you're not comfortable asking for this kind of feedback, then just reflect on what positive qualities others have complimented you on or seem to value in you.

Consider the following questions to help you get in touch with the strengths others see in you:

What have people told you they value about you or that you are good at that can be helpful to keep in mind in difficult social situations?

_____

_____

_____

What personality characteristics and values of yours have people told you that they appreciate?

_____

_____

_____

When you receive compliments, how do you feel?

_____

_____

_____

What things do you do that make people smile?

_____

_____

_____

How have you felt when you've helped friends or family members to see their own strengths at times when they were struggling and perhaps had lost sight of them?

_____

_____

_____

What's something you value about yourself—whether others see it or not?

_____

_____

_____

How can reflecting on the strengths and virtues that others see in you help you see them in yourself?

_____

_____

_____

If you were feeling frustrated at the start of this activity, did your mood improve once you started identifying your strengths?

_____

_____

_____

GRATITUDE TO HELP MANAGE SOCIAL ANGER

The more you value yourself, the less likely it is that you'll feel anger when facing stressful social situations—because you'll know that you can rely on your strengths and other good qualities to see you through hard times. Now let's turn to gratitude, which is another important way that positive psychology can help you manage socially-related anger.

When you appreciate your social connections, you feel more content and less frustrated about what goes on when facing disappointments and struggles. The following tool will help you feel empowered and free of the negative energy and anger you may have about other social situations you may be experiencing.

GETTING PAST SOCIAL ANGER
WITH GRATITUDE

Take a few minutes to remind yourself that gratitude is the ability to appreciate what you value in what goes on around you. When it comes to dealing with letdowns and hardships in your social life, focusing on gratitude with the following questions can help you feel more fulfilled and calmer, preventing you from becoming angry in unproductive ways.

What are one to three things that went well within the last week, socially? For example, it could be that a friend gave you a compliment or asked you to hang out.

_____

_____

_____

How does focusing on this positive social experience help you feel good?

_____

_____

_____

What did you do to help create this positive experience?

_____

_____

_____

What gets in your way of seeing the positive things to be grateful for in your relationships with others?

_____

_____

_____

What can you do to stay aware of social events, interactions, and connections that leave you feeling fulfilled?

_____

_____

_____

MINDFULNESS FOR BODY-IMAGE ANGER

Do you relate to any of the following emotional struggles that may indicate you have anger related to your body image?

- Having negative self-talk or making negative comments about your body.
- Feeling jealous of the bodies of peers or friends or family members.
- Frequently negatively comparing your body to those of others.

If you recognize any of these body-image struggles creating discontent and anger within you, mindfulness can help you find more peace by looking within yourself and around you.

The phrase "body shaming" has become common. It refers to shaming others to feel badly about their bodies. But we can also shame ourselves about our bodies—and this can lead to anger.

BODY-RELATED NEGATIVITY

Reflect mindfully on the body-related words below. Just take a few breaths and notice how you feel after you see them.

Models	Nose	Six-Pack
Skinny	Chest	Thighs
Disgusting	Heavy	Shame
Bloated	Puffy	Embarrassed
Huge	Straight Hair	Flabby
Whale	Wavy Hair	Ugly
Hot	Freckles	Gorgeous
Best Body Part	Zits	Beautiful
Worst Body Part	Pimples	Plain
Best Feature	Gross	Petite
Hairy	Attractive	Ripped
Lean	Loose	Muscular
Arms	Tight Abs	Perfect

As you look at the list above, which body-image words evoke some level of angry feelings for you, and what would be the benefit of letting go of these feelings?

_____

_____

_____

_____

_____

_____

How can your negative associations about these words lead you to miss out on being in the moment to notice your body in a more accepting way?

_____

_____

_____

How does your anger about your body appear to others when you are not mindful to let it go?

_____

_____

_____

What are some things in your life you can mindfully notice in a broader way that are not linked to how you look?

_____

_____

_____

For another way to get yourself out of the confining box of feeling unhealthily consumed with negative energy about your appearance, check out the following tool.

SEEING YOUR BODY
OUT OF THE BOX

Try visualizing your anger related to your body image as a box you are climbing out of. Now imagine seeing your body in an open space. Visualize this space as filled with natural beauty. This could be wildflowers, mountains, blossoming trees, gently flowing streams, the sky, or the ocean. Focus on the sights, sounds, and smells of this new natural beauty that now surrounds you, opening your horizons.

How did it feel to climb out of your restricting body-image box and merge with inspiring images from nature?

_____

_____

How does pondering pleasant images from nature calm you and help you feel more accepting of your body-image concerns?

_____

_____

Once you get out of the box of being locked into judging your appearance, how are you able to feel more positive about how you look?

What situations in your life, if you don't stay mindful, can push you back into that body-image box of negativity that can lead to self-loathing?

_____

_____

Becoming Aware of What's Eating You

Let's mindfully explore a negative way that many people cope with body-image-related frustration and anger—problematic eating.

Have you ever heard someone ask a person who seems annoyed, "What's *eating* you?" This figure of speech describes how our frustration and anger can really consume our attention and distract us from what's going on in the present moment. If you can literally learn to eat mindfully, you can feel more accepting about things that you may struggle with, including anger related to your body image.

Just consider how people sometimes eat on autopilot, without paying attention to their food. Think about how often you eat while doing something else. Have you ever noticed families sitting at a restaurant with parents and kids all absorbed in their phones? These family members are not really focused on truly enjoying their meal, or even each other, for that matter! Some people do three or four things at a time while eating! Mobile devices have certainly made this kind of multitasking very common, and often we are not aware of how much we eat, which can often lead to overeating.

Maybe you believe that eating, in and of itself, or while you're doing something else, like when trying to study or even when relaxing and watching a movie, is a "calm-down reward" that you deserve or just plain want to have. But you will likely value the experience of slowing down. Eating is an important activity, and you can strive to enjoy the experience of eating, not just the sensation of feeling full afterward. Noticing how you experience your food is a great way to gain awareness, which is key to becoming more mindful. It may even help curb overeating when you're stressed.

One cool mindfulness exercise was developed by a well-known mindfulness researcher and practitioner named Jon Kabat-Zinn. It involves mindfully eating a raisin. I love this exercise, because it helps you slow down and pay attention to what is really going on when you lift a bite of food to your mouth. It's like eating with all your senses, not just your sense of taste. Try the following activity to experience eating in perhaps a different way than you ever have before.

MINDFUL AT MEALTIMES

For this activity, you will need a raisin or any food you would like to substitute, such as another piece of fruit, a kernel of popcorn, a piece of gum, a chunk of chocolate, or a small piece of bread. (Whatever you choose, we'll just refer to it as "the raisin.")

1. Sit comfortably in a chair.
2. Place the raisin in the palm of your hand.
3. Examine the raisin with a beginner's mind—as if you had never seen one before.
4. Imagine what the raisin must have looked like when it was a grape growing on a vine. Imagine its plumpness, growing under the sun, surrounded by nature.
5. As you look at the raisin, be conscious of every aspect of what you see: the shape, texture, color, size. Hold the raisin up to the light. Does the raisin look hard or soft, dry or moist?
6. Bring and hold the raisin to your nose. Notice its aroma. Are you anticipating eating the raisin? Is it difficult to resist the temptation to pop it in your mouth?
7. How does the raisin feel in your hand? Gently squeeze the raisin and experience it with your sense of touch.
8. Place the raisin in your mouth. Become aware of how it feels on your tongue.
9. Bite slowly into the raisin. Feel its softness and squishiness (or its hardness and crunchiness).
10. Chew three times and then stop.
11. Notice the flavor of the raisin. What is the texture?
12. Finish chewing, and swallow the raisin. What sensations do you notice as you swallow it?
13. Sit quietly, breathing, aware of what you are sensing as a result of just having swallowed the raisin. Notice how your body and mind are feeling after having completed this mindful eating exercise.

Can you see how being mindful at mealtimes can become an opportunity to reflect on a much broader and deeper experience? A simple piece of food, such as a raisin, is connected to nature. In a way, having grown from a seed, it holds within it all the elements of nature: the earth, wind, rain, and sunshine. And if you eat a salad, a pasta, or other complex dish, you can imagine all the people from around the world who managed the ingredients and put them together. Experiencing your food in a new way, with mindful curiosity, allows you to get back in touch with feeling bigger things in life than your body-image dissatisfaction and related anger. You can feel gratitude and recognize the interconnection of all things.

Try eating mindfully in different places—at home, in the school cafeteria, or in a restaurant. You can even do it in the car—but if you're the one behind the wheel, then please, do it only when parked!

MELT ANGER

WITH HOT CHOCOLATE

The hot (and cool) thing about this exercise is that you can practice breathing and using your senses without focusing on your breath or chewing on a piece of food. If hot chocolate is not appealing to you, try using or imagining hot apple cider, tea, or your favorite soup. This exercise is a brief, easy way to begin exploring mindfulness.

1. Quietly and slowly breathe in through your nose as you smell (or imagine smelling) a mug of hot chocolate.
2. Exhale by blowing through your mouth to cool the beverage off.
3. Repeat the steps four times.

Reflect on how this hot-chocolate breathing exercise was for you.

_____

_____

_____

Could you taste the chocolate with your mind as you breathed in the aroma?

_____

_____

_____

Did it smell pleasurable?

_____

_____

_____

Could you feel yourself cooling the beverage down, as well as blowing away any negative, angry bodily feelings, with your out breath?

_____

_____

_____

SELF-COMPASSION LOWERS BODY-IMAGE ANGER

We have discussed how accepting yourself without judgment is an important part of mindfulness for managing anxiety. This is closely related to the concept of self-compassion, which is about nurturing yourself when you're upset or otherwise hurting emotionally.

Kristin Neff, the founder of the self-compassion movement, points out how we instinctively tend to be really good at giving compassion to the people we value (that is, the people we care about).

When it comes to ourselves, however, it's a different story. Maybe a friend, for example, is upset about having gained weight unexpectedly. Could you easily see yourself giving that friend comfort and encouraging him not to be so hard on himself?

At the same time, though, we often neglect to give ourselves that same type of love and caring. We are really just too hard on ourselves. Becoming angry can actually be a way of punishing yourself over how you look— an unfortunately common, silent struggle. Those harsh, self-directed critical thoughts about your appearance usually make you feel worse. Lacking compassion for yourself in this way just leaves you driving along recklessly on anger avenue.

Self-compassion can help you keep your cool by stopping you from being counterproductively hard on yourself. By embracing compassion for ourselves, we can learn to focus our attention on soothing and taking care of ourselves when we feel upset. Try the next tool to learn self-compassion—putting self-love into your life and seeing how it can help you manage your body-image anger.

ACCEPTANCE WITH
A SELF-COMPASSION HUG

Take a few mindful breaths. On your next in breath, stretch your arms out wide and then bring them in for a big, firm self-hug. Now loosen your arms across your shoulders as you breathe out and then re-embrace yourself more firmly on your next in breath. Repeat this a few times.

How did it feel to warmly accept and nurture yourself in this gentle, caring, affirming way?

_____

_____

_____

What does this tell you about your ability to comfort yourself?

_____

_____

_____

What happens to your self-directed anger when you welcome in self-compassion?

_____

_____

_____

How can you make this self-compassion hug part of your daily life?

_____

_____

_____

CBT FOR BODY-IMAGE ANGER

CBT can help us with body-image anger in many ways. Let's consider the two following examples of body-image-related anger coming from negative comparisons to peers:

Lenny was a devoted fitness guy, waking up each morning at 5:00 a.m. and going to the gym to work out with weights. He met a few friends there and valued the way they'd inspire each other. Lenny felt pleased with the progress he'd made in improving his physique. His friends even gave him positive feedback as he gained muscle mass. One morning, one of his closer friends, Kyle, came into the gym finishing up a muffin, sparking Lenny's recall of Kyle at school eating chips at times. Lenny found himself becoming super angry because he was very careful about his own diet. Unfortunately for Lenny, yet common to most of us, he would find that if he ate less-healthy foods, his body would get softer. Yet he started getting annoyed, thinking, "Kyle can eat anything he wants and look ripped, but I can't. It is so unfair."

Now consider Cayla, a runner who valued keeping fit as well. She found, however, that she was increasingly disturbed and not enjoying her runs as much because she became obsessed with getting her thighs tighter. "After all," she thought, "by now I should have a thigh gap like some of my friends and those hot celebrities."

Following is a tool to help you counter those "should urges" you might have to unfavorably compare your appearance to that of others as Lenny and Cayla did—only creating anger and causing harm. This is not meant as a quick fix, but rather as ongoing practice for a more positive body image.

STOP "SHOULDING"

ANGER ON YOUR BODY

Shoulding can set us up to feel frustrated and angry toward ourselves by sucking us into a trap of negative comparisons to others. Below you will see a series of "shoulds" related to negative body-image comparisons. There is an example that shows how to counter each "should" with a more helpful, reasonable thought.

Fill in the blanks by adding in other ways to counter the "shoulds" that lead to negative body image.

"Should" Body-Image Thought

"Wow, I hate how fat I am! I should be thinner like the other girls I see in the hallways at school."

More Reasonable Body-Image Thought

"I will work toward becoming healthier, but I love myself no matter how my body looks."

"Should" Body-Image Thought

"I should keep up with exercise instead of staying a fat slob."

More Reasonable Body-Image Thought

_____.

"Should" Body-Image Thought

"Damn, my body sucks. In order to be more popular, I should look like the guys that girls think are hot."

More Reasonable Body-Image Thought

_____.

"Should" Body-Image Thought

"I should be happy with my body, but I can't stand it."

More Reasonable Body-Image Thought

_____.

PUTTING IN YOUR
POSITIVE BODY-IMAGE FILTER

Now let's look at another big culprit of counterproductive thinking about body image—negative filtering. If you recall from the list of cognitive distortions on page 36, this counterproductive thinking pattern involves magnifying the negative aspects of something to the extent that it overshadows the positives.

Let's take some of your negative body-image thoughts and replace them with positive thoughts. You can think of this as replacing your negative body-image filter with a positive one.

Negatively Filtered Body-Image Thought

"My nose is so big that no one notices anything else about me."

Positively Filtered Alternative Thought

"Although my nose may be prominent, I am in good shape and also I've been told that I have nice eyes and hair. It helps to realize that I have these other attractive parts of my appearance."

Negatively Filtered Body-Image Thought

"My kinky hair sucks because it ruins my looks."

Positively Filtered Alternative Thought

_____

_____

_____

Negatively Filtered Body-Image Thought

"I have this pudge around my middle—my muffin top—and it makes me totally look like a fat slob."

Positively Filtered Alternative Thought

_____

_____

_____

Negatively Filtered Body-Image Thought

"No matter what I do, I can't get a six pack. I just don't look masculine compared to other guys."

Positively Filtered Alternative Thought

_____

_____

_____

Negatively Filtered Body-Image Thought

"My red hair and freckles make me totally ugly."

Positively Filtered Alternative Thought

_____

_____

_____

POSITIVE PSYCHOLOGY FOR BODY-IMAGE ANGER

Too often we focus on what we want and don't have when it comes to how we look. This can leave us feeling empty and miserable and can trigger us to dwell on what we don't like about ourselves. By focusing more on what you are grateful about your physical self, however, you'll feel less frustrated and angry because you'll feel more fulfilled. This may sound challenging, but you can start just as easily as you would hop into the shower.

GIVING YOUR BODY
A GRATITUDE SHOWER

Simply close your eyes and picture the "good parts" of your body streaming down on you. Notice how satisfying it feels to see the things about your body that you are grateful for. For example, you can be thankful that you have eyes to read or ears to listen. Perhaps you are grateful to have arms to hug your family, friends, or someone else special to you. Maybe you value your legs for the cool hike you took last week. As you notice all the great things about your physical self, your gratitude shower may take longer than you expected because you see even more "good stuff" now that you are opening yourself to noticing it.

How did the image of appreciating positive aspects of your body showering down on you feel to you?

_____

_____

_____

What role does gratitude for your body play in helping you accept the things about it that you struggle with?

_____

_____

_____

How does taking this shower of gratitude help cleanse you of some of the pressuring, all-consuming, anger-soaking body-image thoughts that can make you feel miserable?

_____

_____

_____

What did you learn about your relationship with your body by doing this exercise?

_____

_____

_____

There is nothing wrong with wanting improvements in your life—as long as you don't get too hung up on what you don't have. Now that you've taken a gratitude shower, can you see how being grateful leaves you feeling emotionally fulfilled, whereas being frustrated and self-critical leaves you feeling emotionally empty and upset?

_____

_____

_____

MINDFULNESS FOR FAMILY-RELATED ANGER

Despite the presence of intense feelings, conflicts, and drama between family members, most teens find humor in the fantasy of trading in their parents and siblings for new ones. But it's no laughing matter when family-related frustrations pile up. Let's use mindfulness to bring some calming serenity to the home front during those stormy times that may seem to suddenly blow in from out of nowhere. We have already discussed finding seconds of serenity at school. Since you can use the following tool in pretty much any setting, let's apply it to managing family-related anger.

SEEING SERENITY

IN FAMILY LIFE

The following brief visualizations give you more options for mindfully noticing and letting go of your anger related to family members. You can practice any of these visualizations for as long and as often as you want.

- Visualize bees going from flower to flower. When anger comes up, imagine it initially as a buzzing bee, then watch it buzz more and more softly as it flies farther away until it's out of sight.

- Visualize boxes moving along an assembly line. Each box is a source of your family anger. Use a big rubber stamp to mark each box with an "A" as it goes down the line and out of sight.

- Imagine blowing bubbles with an oversize bubble wand. Each bubble holds something you are angry about. Watch the bubbles float away.

- Imagine your angry thoughts on giant parade floats. Watch them pass you on the street and slowly shrink into the distance.

- Visualize yourself on a lakefront, skipping rocks on the water. Put each frustration on a rock, throw it, and watch it bounce along several times before it sinks.

- Picture your family frustrations as images popping up and fading away on a digital screen.

How do letting go visualizations such as these give you a sense of control by affirmatively letting go of what bothers you?

_____

_____

_____

Were you able to see things more from your family members' point of view?

_____

_____

_____

What are some ways that being less reactive with your emotions might actually result in having less intense and fewer family conflicts?

_____

_____

_____

LETTING RAIN WASH OFF
DIVORCE ANGER

Divorce can lead to feelings of anger for many reasons. If your family or the family of someone you know is experiencing divorce, some common sources of anger are the hard-to-answer questions that result from families undergoing this huge shake-up and change. Thoughts like these are common: "Why is this happening?" or "My parents get what they want but why am I now stuck having to go between two homes?" Let's go back into the RAIN to cope with anger that comes from divorce.

Breathe in and out mindfully a few times. Then step into the RAIN:

Recognize your angry thoughts and feelings and other strong emotions related to your parents' divorce. Are they mostly negative, or are there some positive ones, such as realizing that you don't have to hear your parents quarreling under the same roof anymore, or that you'll have some new opportunities for alone time with each of your parents?

_____

_____

Allow those angry feelings to be present. Don't try to fight or suppress them. As you accept them, notice how you are not being passive and giving in to these feelings or lashing out in response to them. You are just noticing them without judgment, which is a really cool way to manage them.

_____

_____

Inquire and investigate these angry thoughts. What areas of your body do you feel are most affected by your anger? Do you notice your anger as tension? How is noticing your anger without feeling a need to react to it impacting your physical sensations? Does investigating these thoughts, feelings, and sensations give you a sense of clarity?

_____

_____

Not totally defining yourself, asking: "Are my feelings of anger over my parents permanently attached to me, or are they likely to come and go?" Now reflect on these questions and note your feelings:

_____

_____

Do these thoughts and feelings about your parents' divorce have to define you, or can they just be part of you? Describe why.

_____

_____

_____

Does it help to see that anger, like all emotions, will naturally come and go? And while your angry emotions come and go, does it feel centering to know that you are always here? Write your thoughts here.

_____

_____

_____

How did it feel to notice your anger about your parents' divorce in a mindful way?

_____

_____

_____

How can mindfully reflecting on their divorce help you see it in a less upsetting way?

_____

_____

_____

REFRAMING ANGRY THOUGHTS
ABOUT FAMILY MEMBERS

The way you think about family members drives how you feel and behave with them. By using CBT for managing your thoughts, you can have better control of how you manage anger with your family members.

Put a check mark in front of any of the potentially more-helpful ways to reframe your family members:

_____ "She's Lazy." vs. "She struggles at times with motivation."

_____ "He has to be right." vs. "He feels passionate."

_____ "She's a bitch." vs. "She is likely hurting inside."

_____ "He's messed up." vs. "He is probably confused."

_____ "He's a slob." vs. "He has a hard time getting organized."

How helpful could reframing thoughts about family members be in helping you manage anger toward them?

_____

_____

How would you want family members to reframe difficult thoughts about you?

_____

_____

How might your family members respond to you if you judge them less negatively for their challenges and struggles?

_____

_____

What could get in the way of you using reframing to lower anger?

_____

_____

What could you do to promote using this reframing tool in your family where possible?

_____

_____

FAMILY ANGER JOURNAL

By tracing the relationship of your anger-related thoughts, feelings, and behaviors in family situations, you will be better able to understand and manage them. Using the log below is a great way to keep track of the anger-producing family situations that come your way.

Keeping the following log will help you identify thought patterns of your anger at home. Although this tool is for getting a better understanding of your family anger, you can also use this log format to track your anger in other situations, such as at school or with friends. Try to use this log for one to three situations where you experience anger.

FAMILY ANGER LOG

Date and time:_____

What occurred and triggered me?

_____

_____

_____

What was my counterproductive thinking? (For a reference, please see the list of cognitive distortions on page 36.)

_____

_____

_____

What was I feeling?

_____

_____

_____

What was my resulting behavior?

_____

_____

_____

How could I have managed it differently?

_____

_____

_____

In looking over your log, do you see any patterns that emerge regarding your anger over family issues?

_____

_____

_____

Do you think the anger you express in your family could be related to other realms of your life, such as school stress or social situations?

_____

_____

_____

Are there specific patterns related to your anger, such as when you are hungry after school, or rushed and tired in the morning?

_____

_____

_____

In tracking your anger over a few weeks, and feeling more accountable for managing it, can you see it leading to any improvement in how you manage and express anger at home? Explain why.

_____

_____

_____

PUTTING ANGER ASIDE WITH PROBLEM-SOLVING

Problem-solving is an important part of using CBT for anger management. You can use problem-solving to work through anger by taking a reasonable look at what the problem is in a given situation and then generating possible solutions. Let's say you really want to hang out at a friend's house this Saturday afternoon and then sleep over there, but your parents want you to stay home for the weekend to do some yard work and be together as a family. Assuming there is no magic potion available to offer your parents to drink and instantly get them onboard with you going to see your friend on your terms alone, explore the following tool for an example of how to problem-solve this situation.

PROBLEM-SOLVING
ANGER AT YOUR PARENTS

The following is a commonly used five-step model for problem-solving: (1) identify the problem, (2) think of possible steps to take, (3) consider the consequences of the proposed solutions, (4) implement a solution, and (5) monitor the effectiveness of the chosen solution. By thinking through the steps needed for good problem-solving, you may avoid the impulsive "Go, Set, Ready" trap we first mentioned earlier when we discussed mindful texting.

1. Identify the problem. Start by noticing what you're angry about and why, and try to describe it. You may ask yourself: "What's got me angry? What am I feeling, and why?" In this current example, you are angry that your parents are limiting the time you want to spend seeing your friend this weekend. You might put this into words by telling yourself: "My parents are restricting my sense of freedom by telling me that I need to stay home, and this interferes with seeing my friend. It's not fair!" You're feeling angry, therefore, because you might not get to go see your friend, and you feel this is unjust. Your angry thought here is quite different from simply thinking, "They are so unfair to me!" This statement doesn't identify the specific problem (that you can't see your friend because your parents want you to do chores and stick around the house), and it doesn't specifically say how you're feeling (angry).

2. Think of potential actions (before responding). Thinking in a constructive way about what you may want to say or how you want to react gives you time to manage your anger. In our current example, this could mean asking yourself, "What can I offer?" Then think of at least three suggestions. For example, in this situation you might think: (a) I could manipulatively start crying or aggressively scream at my parents and throw a fit. (b) I could begin cleaning my room and take out the trash from the kitchen, and then after demonstrating positive intentions, I could politely ask if there is some amended time frame we could work with so that I can still go to my friend's house. (c) I could sneak out to my friends on my terms.

3. Think through the likely consequences of each solution. This is where you consider the likely result from each of the different actions you came up with. Ask yourself: What will happen after each one of these options? For example: (a) Trying to manipulate or be verbally aggressive toward your parents will likely backfire, leading to negative energy and you being put in an even more restrictive situation. (b) Cleaning your room takes work and taking out the trash takes time, and your parents may still not agree to bend in letting you see your friend. But the chances of their reconsidering will be higher because you've been cooperative and created positive energy. With this option, you have a better chance of being able to spend some time with your friend, and you can also feel like you're doing your part in meeting family responsibilities. (c) Sneaking out, when you really think it through, will almost certainly mean an escalation of the conflict with your parents (vs. progress toward resolving it)!

4. Decide (pick one of your options). At this point, you consider the options and pick the one that is likely to be most workable. Ask yourself: What's my best choice? Now that you've thought it through, you're probably past option (a), wanting to act out with your parents by manipulating or screaming in a fit of anger, which is an impulsive and ineffective "Go, Set, Ready" response. You likely also decided that option (c), sneaking out, just isn't worth it and will only make things worse. Neither of these options is likely to get your parents to agree to letting you spend some time with your friend. So option (b) probably seems like the best choice.

5. Monitor for Effectiveness. After you've acted on the chosen option, give it some reflection. Ask yourself: "How did it go? Did this work out as I expected? If not, why not? Am I satisfied with the choice I made?" Reflecting in this way helps you learn about yourself and what works and doesn't work in managing potential anger-sparking conflicts with your parents.

These five problem-solving steps are pretty simple when you're calm, but are much tougher to work through when you're angry or sad (just like making your shots in basketball practice is likely much easier than in a real game when the pressure is on!). So it helps to practice over and over again. Let's start problem-solving practice for family-related anger with the following questions:

In what recent conflict could this problem-solving approach have helped you?

_____

_____

_____

What are some potential solutions for this problem?

_____

_____

_____

How can you evaluate the possible success of these options as possible solutions?

_____

_____

_____

Pick a possible solution to use for this situation.

_____

_____

_____

How can you monitor its effectiveness?

_____

_____

_____

Now that you have taken these problem-solving steps, reflect on your counterproductive reactions. How can they get in the way of working through conflicts with family members?

_____

_____

_____

Can you see how proactively evaluating your reactions and behaviors with a "Ready, Set, Go" mindset promotes better control of your thoughts and feelings when you are angry?

_____

_____

_____

What can you do to help yourself use this problem-solving approach in the future?

_____

_____

_____

POSITIVE PSYCHOLOGY FOR FAMILY ANGER

Discovering our strengths when it comes to managing anger within our families sometimes means looking at what we have done at least fairly well in the past to overcome difficult situations. The term "selective attention" refers to how our brains pay attention to only some of the many things to see in our environment. Anger can narrow your focus, making your attention even more selective, causing you to focus on anger-provoking situations that did not turn out well. For example, if your older sibling playfully teases you and you end up giving it back in ways where your anger gets out of control, then you may lose sight of being able to have some laughs with your sibling.

In this case with your older sibling, you may unfairly only label them as "annoying" and yourself as an overreactor. If this is the case, you make it even easier for your brain to "go there" (to anger) when you and your sibling interact.

In this case with your sibling, can you see how selective attention can lead to negative labeling? A way out of negatively labeling yourself is to look at exceptions to the label. In the case of managing your anger, the more you consider those situations that you handle well, the less you will label yourself negatively in those situations. Check out the following tool to learn how to take those times when you handled anger well in the past and apply them in the future with your family.

PAYING FORWARD

BEST FAMILY ACTIONS

Recall a time when you were angry with a family member but you handled it fairly well. Reflect on how, at the time, maybe it felt like you were at your wits' end and perhaps your anger level got high, even furious. Maybe a sibling accidentally broke something that meant a lot to you. Perhaps your parents seemed to unfairly jump to a mistaken conclusion.

What did you do in this situation that helped you manage your anger more successfully than at other times?

_____

_____

_____

How does noticing this better instance of coping make you feel as you reflect on it?

_____

_____

_____

How could realizing your success at the time have helped you learn?

_____

_____

_____

Can you see how we may unfairly limit ourselves when it comes to anger management in thinking only about learning from our mistakes vs. learning from our successes as well? Explain your thoughts.

_____

_____

_____

Reflect on past coping strategies used in anger-provoking situations. How did it help you better manage your anger going forward?

_____

_____

_____

FINDING FAMILY GRATITUDE
AND LOSING ANGER

Anger leaves us feeling drained and depleted, while feeling grateful puts us in a place of feeling fulfilled. Now let's look at how having gratitude with your family can help you manage your anger with them.

Reflect on the following questions and consider how they can lower your anger toward family members or family situations.

What are three things you are grateful for in your family that feel calming when you focus on them?

_____

_____

_____

How could focusing on gratitude for and within your family help provide you with an opportunity to lower angry feelings when you're around them?

_____

_____

_____

Can you see how the more you focus on what you appreciate about family members, the easier it becomes to do so?

_____

_____

_____

What might block you from focusing on what you are grateful for in your family and how can you stop this block from limiting you?

_____

_____

_____

What positive effect could you have by inspiring yourself and your family to focus on the good stuff and appreciate it?

_____

_____

HANDLING ANXIETY, COPING WITH DEPRESSION, AND MANAGING ANGER FOR LIFE

Congratulations for making it to the end of this book. Keep in mind that modern teens, in our fast-paced, digital age, may be under more pressure and stress than any other generation of youth in recent history. Believe me when I say that by comparison, your parents had it easy!

Whether you'll soon be super worried about an upcoming test, or sad because someone you thought of as a good friend is pulling away, or you're angry seeing that you're now being left out of group texts, or your social media feed isn't getting the "likes" it used to, you likely have a lot on your plate. Adding to all of this, maybe your well-intentioned parents keep asking you questions but just don't seem to understand what makes you tick. To be totally fair, maybe *you're* still trying to figure out what makes you tick.

As you go through tough times, you will have thoughts, feelings, and behaviors related to anxiety, depression, and anger. Remember, though, that your goal is to manage—not to stop—having these emotions. By using the coping skills you've learned through the tools in this book, you will be better able to manage emotional struggles at school, successfully navigate your social relationships, appreciate your physical self in a more supportive and positive way, and be able to cope with family struggles.

Most important, by learning about how to cope with troubling emotions, you will be better able to enjoy the good times, and you'll have super-effective ways to cope with those down times, too. Feel proud of yourself for having the willingness to learn these critically important coping skills for life.

KEEP WORKING AT IT

Even though you now have some really good coping skills, you might still sometimes find yourself trying to avoid challenging emotions by streaming too many videos, passing a bit too much time on social media, or playing an excessive number of games on your phone every chance you get. Maybe you'll lash out at your parents (or your brother or sister) without meaning to (after all, you're only human, right?). Perhaps you will strongly vent about your feelings to your friends, but after a while they may not seem to want to listen anymore, which will be frustrating in itself. Or maybe you'll just want to sleep so that you don't have to deal with anyone or anything.

But even if you fall back into some not-so-healthy ways of coping with the challenges that come your way, just remember that the tools and activities you have learned in this book are always available to you—for the rest of your life, in fact. The more you use them, the better you'll feel.

There's lots of fun to be had as a teenager. So as you go back out there and enjoy the exciting experiences and opportunities opening up for you, I'll leave you with the inspiring words of one of my really cool-to-work-with teen clients:

> It's weird, man. I just realized that getting all kinds of worried, being down, and pissed all the time wasn't working for me. When I started dealing with what was going on in my head, my friends noticed me being calmer and happier. They asked me to show them the stuff that helped me, and it felt really cool to help them.

So there you have it. Helping others you see struggling to learn to use what you've learned can lead them to feeling better. And this can further keep you inspired to stay on your own path of calming down, facing challenges, and enjoying your life!

Part D

A GUIDE FOR THERAPISTS

TO PROMOTE MAXIMUM EFFECTIVENESS OF ALL THE TOOLS

To help ensure that teens have the best buy-in (and results) from the tools presented in this workbook, this section describes ways to set them up for success, respond to discouragement, and handle setbacks. These final pages, while primarily for therapists and other professionals, also provide further valuable information for teens and their parents.

BE REAL WHEN MEETING RESISTANCE

If teens are resistant to trying out any tools, let them know you value their resistance rather than letting them work half-heartedly on these tools with you in session, or say they will do them outside of session and then not follow through. For dealing with their resistance, you can then say something to them like this:

> *I hear you. There are days when I am just not into doing things like this, either. The last thing I want to do is "should" on you—by telling you why you should do these activities with me. At the same time, I really do think they can help you, if you are willing to give one or two a try. Maybe you can even sit back and watch me do one or two of these, just so you can get a sense of them.*

If the teen engages at this point, then you are in. If the teen is still resistant, you could say something like the following:

> *If you are not feeling this right now, how about we listen to some songs or check out a favorite website you like or take a walk or play a card game? Then, afterward maybe we can talk about how aspects of listening to the music or looking at the website or taking a walk are absorbing, mindful experiences that might even tie into some of the other stuff in this workbook. Are you cool with that?*

If teens say they will try using the tools between sessions and then they don't follow through, be empathetic and explore what factors got in the way of them practicing.

For example, some teens with high levels of anxiety, sadness, or anger may express that "nothing will work for me." Therefore, when introducing any of the interventions in this workbook to teens who are more skeptical, it helps to be low-key with prompts such as:

> *"How about we give this a try?"* vs. *"It is important for you do this exercise if you want to feel better."*

In short, if your clients are resistant to the tools in this workbook, go with their resistance (as discussed above) rather than challenging it. Otherwise you will likely trigger a rigid "That does not/will not work for me" type of comment, where they prematurely dismiss the potential value of the interventions.

Another important consideration when managing client resistance is that sometimes teens may be unwilling to try something during one session but may be more open to doing so next time, or the time after, so patience on your part can really pay off. Also, realize that the unique structure of this workbook offers a wide variety of interventions for clients who favor mindfulness, CBT, positive psychology, or any combination thereof.

MANAGE YOUR CLIENTS' EXPECTATIONS

Whether your clients buy in right away or you help them work through their resistance to doing so, help them go gradually when learning these strategies, and promote realistic expectations so that your clients avoid getting discouraged. Help them so they don't just mechanically try out the tools or do them hastily or half-heartedly only to try to convince you or themselves that they don't work. Be a self-assured conveyor of the message that "These well-researched tools do work—if *you* work at using them."

To further encourage your clients to have healthy expectations for getting results and feeling better, you may want to explain about the cool, relatively recent concept in psychology called *neuroplasticity*. To introduce this concept, you could say something like this:

> *Psychologists used to think that our neurological makeup was more or less established in childhood and, after that, we were stuck with particular ways of thinking, feeling, and acting. But now we know that these connections aren't set in stone. In the same way that plastic can be reformed, reshaped, or remolded, our brains can be rewired. By putting in effort to overcome our challenges and unhelpful habits, we can create new, more helpful neural connections and strengthen them through practice. Then our old ways of thinking, feeling, and behaving become weaker and less automatic. In the beginning, it's easy to fall back into our old ways, but, as time goes on, our new ways can become second nature. And this applies when using the tools in this book. The more we practice them and give them a chance, the more effective we will find them to be.*

To help further convey this concept of neuroplasticity (e.g., change coming with practice and time), you could say something similar to this to your teen client:

> *Imagine that for some years you've been walking through a grassy field in a consistent way, and your footsteps have worn a path—the path of facing emotional struggles without having tools to cope with them. Even though the terrain is difficult—you have to climb over rocks and through slippery mud, and sometimes risk twisting your ankle on the bumpy ground—it seemed to be the only way of making your way through. But now, having read this workbook and taken the concepts to heart, you've begun to walk through that field by a different route. You've created a new path for coping with stress. This road is much smoother, and the obstacles seem smaller and easier to handle.*
>
> *Yes, at times it may not feel easy to stay on this new path. Maybe peers around you are walking around saying negative things or not making the best choices in response to struggling with difficult feelings. You may feel pulled toward them and start to go back down that old, familiar path of walking in circles, consumed by troublesome thoughts and feelings that lead you right back to feeling like you are hopelessly hurting without any relief available. But as shown in this book, there are many alternative helpful paths to take to feeling better. All it takes is the willingness to find the paths that seem like good ones for you.*

You may be wondering, "Yeah, all that sounds good, but what if a teen hears all this neuroplasticity and practice-over-time stuff, and still comes back a week or so later and says that the strategies are not helpful out of session?" This is a valid concern. Many teens who seem engaged in therapeutic activities in counseling sessions and acknowledge finding value in them may then later report that the strategies don't really help them after all. When you find yourself in this position with a client, the following section may be of help.

HOW TO RESPOND TO "THIS HASN'T HELPED ME"

Usually when teens report that interventions don't work for them to help them manage their emotions, it is due to any of these three reasons:

1. They aren't practicing.
2. They are practicing somewhat, but they are still rigidly locked into counterproductive behavior patterns (e.g., avoidance when feeling anxious, isolation when feeling depressed, lashing out when angry) that undermine the practice.
3. They are practicing but it hasn't been very long, and they are expecting results prematurely.

To help empower teens to practice the tools in this book, it may help to bring in the comparison of getting better in sports (or other activities, such as playing an instrument or dancing) through practice. Doing this can help manage their expectations and promote more of their investment in being patient and putting in the time. For example, you could say something like this:

> *Let's say that you're the coach, and your players come back and says that they aren't getting better—or your guys lose the game and then they say that your coaching isn't working. What would you say? Maybe they didn't practice . . . or maybe not enough (it takes time to build "muscle memory"), or maybe they are doing something to undermine their performance. In sports, this would be overthinking rather than being in the moment, or daydreaming, etc.*

> *Continuing with this example, if a player didn't practice and said that he didn't intend to practice, what would you do? (Maybe discuss whether he is committed to the team or might want to wait for another season and try it again.) If he was practicing, but not enough, what would you do? (Maybe advise him to be patient and keep practicing, maybe get some extra coaching, like from a parent, etc.). Let's take a look at what's happening in your situation.*

The other point to share with clients who claim not to benefit from these interventions is acceptance. If they think that the goal is to get rid of the troublesome emotion, you'll have to tell them that this is simply not correct. It's commonly estimated that our brains have about 2,500 thoughts per hour, and 50,000 to 70,000 thoughts per day. This would be a really cool tidbit to share with them.

You can also tie in the beachball metaphor to convince them that it's just impossible to stop our thoughts. That would be like trying to hold a beachball underwater. It will keep popping up.

Acceptance suggests that the goal for all of us is to live our lives in spite of anxious, sad, or angry emotions and accept that they come and go, no matter what tools we have in place. Paradoxically, once that acceptance is there, the feelings of not being able to manage emotions go away. One client said at the end of counseling, "I got control of my emotions by letting them be there."

Set a No-Homework Policy

Try to avoid calling it "homework" when encouraging teens to practice the skills you help them learn from this workbook. The word *homework* can understandably have a negative connotation with teens. Who would really want to even hear this term at all? Ugh! This is especially the case since counseling sessions are usually during after-school hours. Many teens come to counseling sessions feeling tired or burned out from a long school day. If you become another discriminative stimulus that they'll associate with their teacher at school giving them homework to do, the risk of them mentally checking out becomes much higher.

Manage Setbacks Supportively

Many teens who do make progress using the tools in this workbook may get discouraged or feel hopeless down the line if they hit a setback. In situations where teens have made some progress but then become discouraged, or struggle in some other way when experiencing setbacks, you could say something like this:

> *Yes, it would be great for all of us to stay on top of upsetting thoughts every single time. But our daily lives are filled with distractions and time pressures that make it easy to get swept along by lots of upsetting thoughts and feelings. So keep in mind that just because you may feel at times like the walls are closing in or that you're spinning out of control on the inside, that still doesn't mean you can't use your tools. Just as you now know that you don't have to be perfect, know too that you don't have to use your strategies perfectly or get great results all the time for them to be valuable.*

> *And if you ever start to think, "I just can't handle my emotions! I tried mindfulness, CBT skills, and positive psychology, but they don't work for me," remember that learning to manage your thoughts and feelings takes practice. John Eliot, a psychologist and author of Overachievement, is known for these words of wisdom: "Thinking is a habit, and like any other habit it can be changed; it just takes effort and repetition." The more you identify your counterproductive coping patterns and replace them with more reasonable, helpful thoughts, the calmer and happier you'll feel. You'll also make wiser decisions because you'll be using your thinking brain instead of your reactive brain.*

Pointers for Using Mindfulness with Teens

The more you demystify mindfulness, the more teens can realize that it is a skill they can begin to practice right away. To help teens understand this, you could say:

> *You already have the rich, powerful benefits of mindfulness. Think about moments of joy in your life when you really noticed what was around you. At those times, you were being mindful by being aware of what was going on in the present moment.*

> *Here are some examples. Have you ever …*

- *watched a beautiful, peaceful sunset and felt it was a magical experience?*
- *walked outside and loved the feeling of the gentle breeze or the warm sun on your skin?*
- *petted a dog or a cat and been fully absorbed in the exchange of affection?*
- *listened to music and felt emotionally and spiritually moved, as though you were part of the music?*
- *hung out with friends and felt as though the time just melted away?*
- *cleaned your room and felt so "in the groove" while cleaning that you were amazed at how much you got done?*
- *did just one thing at a time and felt super focused?*

You can further explain mindfulness to teens in this way:

> *There are two ways to practice mindfulness. Informal practice involves having a moment-to-moment awareness of things like really feeling the gentle, warm breeze when you're walking outside. It's a way to be mindful as you go about your usual activities. You don't have to watch a beautiful sunset or listen to wonderful music to informally practice mindfulness. In fact, being mindful while doing run-of-the-mill, "boring" daily activities can help you appreciate the best parts of these experiences. To get a clue as to what I'm talking about, the next time you brush*

your teeth, focus on the pleasant, refreshing feeling of having a cleaner mouth. Or do any of the following:

- *Take a shower, focusing on the warmth and comforting flow of the cleansing water.*
- *Text a friend, focusing on how cool this form of instant communication is.*
- *Play an instrument, focusing on the magic of creating musical sound.*
- *Draw a picture, focusing on watching your own creative energy in action as you bring an image to life.*
- *Exercise, focusing on really feeling the exertion of your body and mind.*

Doing any everyday activity with a more focused awareness may bring you a little more joy or lighten your spirit.

Then you can add:

The activities in this workbook will not only strengthen your informal practice of mindfulness but also teach you how to do it a second way, as a formal practice. A formal practice involves actually setting aside time to be mindful. To prepare, you find a quiet space, sit in a relaxed position, and, if you like, close your eyes. (Unless otherwise instructed, please follow these guidelines whenever using the mindfulness tools in this workbook.)

Related to this, make another important point to teens::

Mindfulness is called a "practice" for a reason—the more you do it, the better you'll get at it. Don't be intimidated or get discouraged when practicing seems hard. Don't pressure yourself to be perfect at using mindfulness.

Explaining Why Mindfulness Helps Manage Difficult Emotions

Share with your teen clients that when they have mindful moments, they are not likely tuned in to their consuming emotions. You could say something like this:

A mindful moment with your friends may involve feeling really captivated by what your friends are saying. A mindful moment when you're walking outside may involve gazing in wonderment at the sparkling heavens. When you start heading home on the school bus and look back at your school growing smaller in the distance, maybe you feel only a fantastic sense of freedom. Maybe you're mindful of that similar feeling of letting go after getting off work at your part-time job and driving away in your car, or catching a ride with a friend. When you're focused on the good things in life, your worries seem to fade.

Whether you are having an unplanned mindful moment or doing one of the mindfulness exercises in this workbook, remember that in the same way that you can't be hot when you are cold, or go fast when you are going slow, it's really not possible to be worried, sad, or angry when you are mindfully relaxed. No longer will you honestly be able to say, "I can't control my emotions." How cool would that be? Instead of having your head overwhelmed with challenging emotions that you feel you need to react to, mindfulness can take you to a better place.

Making a Case for Mindfulness in a World of Digital Devices

Your teen clients, like all of us to some extent, are likely immersed in our digital world, which is filled with absorbing and soothing distractions, making it challenging to mindfully tune in to themselves or others. Given this intense competition for attention and time, the like of which we have never faced before this digital age, it is helpful to have teens understand that the mindfulness exercises, as the others in this workbook, do not require much time. One way to express this important point to your clients is this:

Have you wondered what it would be like to put down those screens for brief periods (or even longer, if you are willing) and take some mindfulness breaks to calm and recharge your highly-stimulated mind? If you don't like to put your digital devices too far out of reach, guess what? I have some good news for you! Believe it or not, the digital world can be a great facilitator and means of engaging in the world of mindfulness. Here are some ways you can turn your electronics from hindrances into helpers:

- *You can use texting, Snapchat®, Instagram®, WhatsApp®, Facebook®, Tumblr®, Twitter®, Reddit®, or any other social media platform to capture cool pictures of nature scenes and share or post them.*

- *You can check out the growing number of YouTube® videos that provide mindfulness exercises and activities. These include breathing exercises, visualizations, soothing sounds, yoga activities, and guided meditations.*

- *You may also want to explore the expanding world of mindfulness apps in order to reinforce skills you have learned in this workbook and also to learn new ones. There are some wonderful gratitude apps, breathing apps, yoga apps, and meditation apps. Breathe2Relax, Calm, Insight Timer, and Smiling Mind are some mindfulness apps that many teens really like.*

CONSIDERATIONS FOR USING CBT WITH TEENS

Explain to your clients that CBT is a counseling approach that helps people identify the thoughts and beliefs (in this workbook, I often use the terms *thoughts* and *beliefs* interchangeably) that are upsetting them or stressing them out. Emphasize that a big part of *how* we experience certain events (e.g., at a very basic level, whether an event is "good" or "bad") is influenced by *our thoughts* about them (Beck, 2018). In other words, what we believe those events *mean*—about us, other people, the future, and so on—has a huge influence on how we feel about them.

To further help teens understand the basics of CBT, you could say something like this:

Having negative thoughts about a difficult situation is normal. No one can stay positive all the time. And you can't force yourself to stop having unhelpful, upsetting thoughts. But if you let your reactive brain fuel those thoughts, they can spiral out of control. Can you visualize how a funhouse mirror, rather than reflecting you as you really are, warps and twists your image, making you appear distorted from your true self? Similarly, your reactive brain distorts your thoughts, and this can lead you to assume that a given situation is hopeless or that you're headed for disaster. As a result, you may do things that don't really help, which can ultimately become destructive patterns in your life or leave you anxious, unhappy, or angry. You can, however, train your thinking brain to have stronger, helpful thoughts that can counter your reacting brain's upsetting and unhelpful thoughts! Your helpful thoughts about situations can lead you to better feelings and better outcomes.

The Cycle of Thoughts, Feelings, and Actions

A graphic such as the one below can help teens visualize how the thoughts we have influence the feelings we have, and how the feelings we have influence our actions. Then our actions influence the thoughts we have later, and so on. This diagram illustrates how negative thoughts, feelings, and actions occur in a cyclical manner. You can draw this in front of them on a sheet of paper.

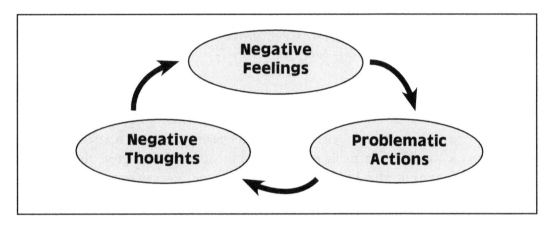

As you show teens this diagram, you could say something like:

> *As you can see from the diagram, according to the CBT model, negative thoughts drive negative feelings, which lead to problematic actions. If you don't interrupt the cycle, you can get locked into a spiral of anxiety, doom and gloom, or anger.*

Below are two concrete examples of teen situations that can give teen clients an idea of how CBT works in real life:

Example 1

Let's say you recently changed schools, and you're looking for a place to sit in the cafeteria at lunchtime. You spot a girl you've said hi to in the hallways, but she's sitting with a group of people you've never met. You think: "I'd like to go sit at that table, but they'll probably reject me"—which makes you anxious and discouraged. As a result, you choose to sit at an empty table (withdrawing/avoiding behavior), letting this chance to connect with a potential group of friends pass you by (and ensuring that you remain lonely yet another day).

CBT skills can help you identify, challenge, and replace your unhelpful or counterproductive thoughts, feelings, and actions. In the cafeteria example, you could reframe the situation and try thinking about things differently. In response to the thought, "They'll probably reject me," you could argue, "They do seem cool, though, and I do kind of know a few of them." That might help you feel more confident about going to their table, and you'll likely feel really good about yourself for taking this important step to expand your friend group.

Example 2

Imagine that you arrive in your first-period classroom and sit down as usual. Then the teacher announces that it's time to discuss the assignment that you forgot to submit last night through the school's online portal. You feel your face turning red. You beat yourself up over this embarrassing situation with thoughts like, "I suck at life!" "I just can't manage anything right!" You shut down and decide not to do the assignment at all, even though you're still responsible for completing it. As a result, you'll receive a zero, and you might get a poor grade in the class, which won't sit well with you or your parents. Now imagine that you look at the situation in a less self-critical way and say to yourself: "Everyone makes mistakes. Yes, I am frustrated right now, but I'll discuss this with my teacher and work hard and quickly to make this assignment up."

The main points to convey to teens are that by using CBT skills when they struggle with difficult feelings, they can learn to identify the counterproductive thoughts that pop up in their minds, evaluate them, and respond to them. You can further encourage teen clients by saying the following:

By practicing at generating better, healthier thoughts, you'll be in a great position to manage stress and to be more successful when facing challenges.

What to Say When Teens Can't Say

In the examples above, it was assumed that the teens knew exactly what was bothering them. As a therapist, however, you've likely had, and will have, teens who describe feeling anxious, stressed, sad, or angry for no apparent reason in particular. This is actually quite normal for teens. What's great about CBT skills is that you don't have to try to figure out what happened or who's to blame. You can start to help them by exploring areas of their lives that are going well and those not going so well.

You can say something like this to your client who has strong upsetting emotions and is unable to link them to thought patterns:

Let's pretend that I am throwing wet spaghetti on your refrigerator. Some pieces will stick and some won't. Let's make a list of the things that are going well, and another list of the things that are going not so well. I will help you. Now that we see more closely what has been happening in your life, can you see how some of these that aren't going so well may lead you to think certain things?

At this point, you can show the teen the list of cognitive distortions first presented on page 36 of this workbook. Then help your client identify which cognitive distortions may be occurring and go from there in exploring the CBT model. End with reinforcing that CBT skills can put *them* in charge of their thoughts, feelings, and behaviors!

A PRIMER FOR USING POSITIVE PSYCHOLOGY WITH TEENS

Positive psychology is about helping your clients see their strengths, meet challenges in order to feel good about themselves, gain gratitude, and develop an optimistic outlook. CBT and positive psychology both share a central belief that you can use the way you *think* to help yourself *feel* better.

It appears that positive psychology has been neglected in the mental health field. The following quotation from famous psychologist Abraham Maslow (1908–1970) suggests that although psychology has historically focused on people's limitations and internal struggles, we can also use psychology to focus on the things we like about ourselves and the "good stuff" in our lives.

The science of psychology has been far more successful on the negative than on the positive side. It has revealed to us much about man's shortcomings, his illnesses, his sins, but little about his potentialities, his virtues, his achievable aspirations, or his full psychological height. It is as if psychology has voluntarily restricted itself to only half its rightful jurisdiction . . . the darker, meaner half. -Maslow (1954, page 354)

Positive psychology is a way to foster hope and work through stress by focusing on the things that are going well in one's life. It can guide your teen clients to recognize their strengths, practice optimism, gain grit, get into a state of flow, and stay grateful for the good things in their lives.

Some clients have misunderstandings about positive psychology, thinking that it means "just be happy" all the time and then your problems will magically disappear. They associate positive psychology with people who constantly smile as though they don't have a worry in the world—but no one like this truly exists. Help your clients understand that positive psychology does not involve memorizing special scripts that will program their brains to be immune to challenging situations and emotions.

To insure your clients benefit from positive psychology, you can reinforce that it will help them:

- See their inner strengths and talents.
- Think in more optimistic ways to help face their challenges and succeed.
- Develop grit to persevere and find a way through setbacks and disappointments.
- Get "in the zone" and be in a state of joy while absorbed in what they're doing.
- See that being more thankful helps them be happier.

When working with your clients on positive psychology interventions, it is also important that they realize that positive psychology is not:

- A set of self-brainwashing techniques to make them superior to others.
- Thinking that happy, positive thoughts guarantee positive outcomes.
- Being able to completely eliminate adversity and prevent tough times.
- Expecting activities to be automatically rewarding.
- Assuming they'll automatically feel happier by having more good things in their lives.
- Training themselves to be effortlessly satisfied and happy all the time.

MANAGING PARENTS

Sometimes well-meaning parents unwittingly put pressure on their children and teens in the counseling process. They may ask after a session, "What did you talk about?" Or parents may ask things between sessions such as: "How are you doing? Are your skills working? Are you still anxious? Or are you practicing what you did in your counseling sessions?"

To help set boundaries with parents, and at the same time, be supportive to them, you could say something like this:

> *My work is to support your teen's emotional health. This involves your child feeling safe sharing their concerns with me confidentially. While your child will always remain your child, this is a time of development and change for your teen when they are looking for self-worth, purpose, and a sense of identity and direction for the future.*
>
> *It is my hope that in order to help maximize the chances of your child getting the most out of the counseling process, you as the parents respect the confidentiality between your teen and me. Therefore, I suggest that you avoid questioning your child about the specifics discussed during sessions. Of course, I encourage teen clients to share important information and feelings with you. If a situation arises that I feel is necessary for you to be informed about, I will arrange a meeting for your teen and you to discuss the pertinent issues.*

REFERENCES

"11 facts about anxiety." (2019). DoSomething.org. Retrieved from https://www.dosomething.org/us/facts/11-facts-about-anxiety.

Beck, J. (2018). *Definition of CBT* (video). Psychwire. Available from https://psychwire.com/beck/resources/definition-of-cbt.

Bernstein, J. (2017). *Letting go of anger—Card deck for teens.* Eau Claire, WI: PESI Publishing.

Bernstein, J. (2017). *Letting go of teen worry.* Oakland, CA: New Harbinger Publications.

Bernstein, J. (2019). *The stress survival guide for teens.* Oakland, CA: New Harbinger Publications.

Brach, T. (2016, January 13). Feeling overwhelmed? Remember "RAIN." *Mindful.* Retrieved from http://www.mindful.org/tara-brach-rain-mindfulness-practice.

Dealing with anger. (2015). KidsHealth. TeensHealth. Retrieved from https://kidshealth.org/en/teens/deal-with-anger.html.

Holland, J. (2015, March 9). Grit: The key ingredient to your kids' success. *On Parenting* (blog). *Washington Post.* Retrieved from https://www.washingtonpost.com/news/parenting/wp/2015/03/09/grit-the-key-ingredient-to-your-kids-success.

Maslow, A. (1954). *Harper's Psychological Series.* New York, NY: Harper.

Siegel, D. (2010). *Mindsight: The New Science of Personal Transformation.* New York, NY: Bantam Books.

Strong, D. (2015). 7 ways anger is ruining your health. *Everyday Health.* Retrieved from https://www.everydayhealth.com/news/ways-anger-ruining-your-health/.

Teenage anger. (2018). Psych Central. Retrieved from https://psychcentral.com/lib/teenage-anger/.

Teen depression. (2018). WebMD. Retrieved from https://www.webmd.com/depression/guide/teen-depression.

Todd, J., Aspell, J. E., Barron D., and Swami, V. (June 2019). Multiple dimensions of interoceptive awareness are associated with facets of body image in British adults. *Body Image* 29, 6–16. DOI: 10.1016/j.bodyim.2019.02.003.

Made in the USA
Las Vegas, NV
22 April 2022